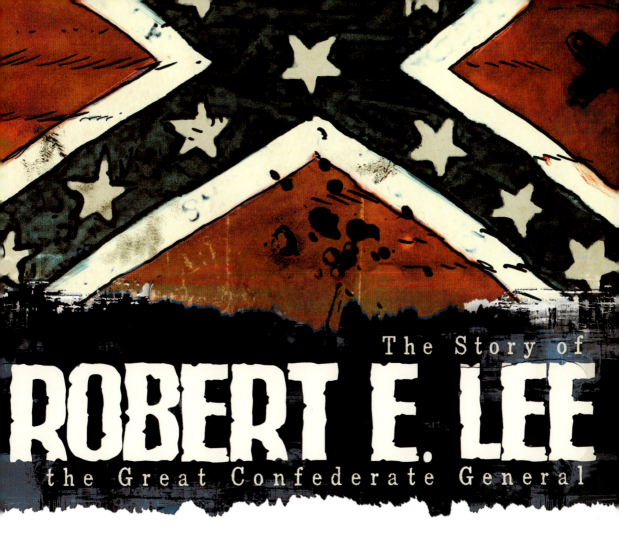

The Story of
ROBERT E. LEE
the Great Confederate General

by Terry Collins

illustrated by Cristian Mallea

Consultant:
Tim Solie
Adjunct Professor of History
Minnesota State University, Mankato

CAPSTONE PRESS
a capstone imprint

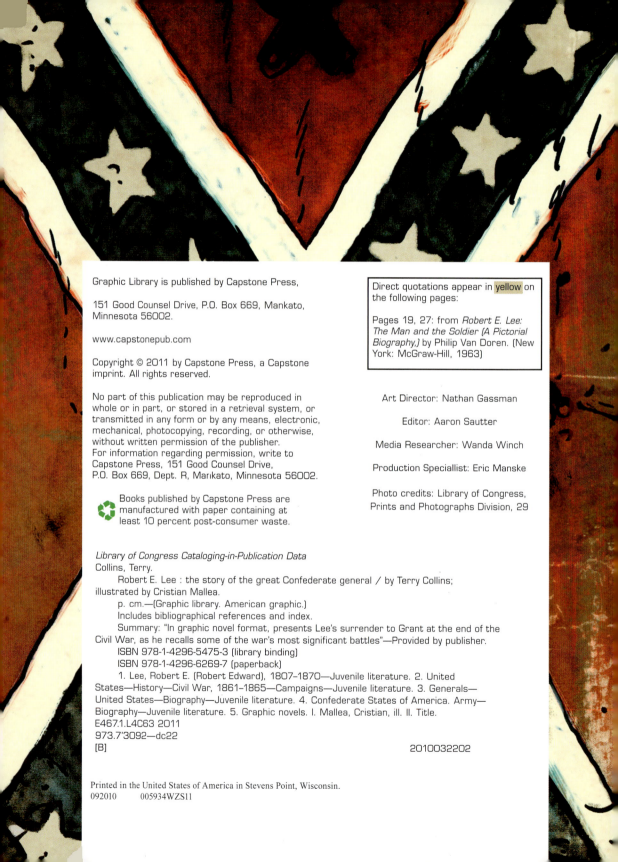

Graphic Library is published by Capstone Press,

151 Good Counsel Drive, P.O. Box 669, Mankato,
Minnesota 56002.

www.capstonepub.com

Books published by Capstone Press are
manufactured with paper containing at
least 10 percent post-consumer waste.

Direct quotations appear in yellow on
the following pages:

Pages 19, 27: from *Robert E. Lee:
The Man and the Soldier (A Pictorial
Biography,)* by Philip Van Doren. (New
York: McGraw-Hill, 1963)

Art Director: Nathan Gassman

Editor: Aaron Sautter

Media Researcher: Wanda Winch

Production Specialist: Eric Manske

Photo credits: Library of Congress,
Prints and Photographs Division, 29

Library of Congress Cataloging-in-Publication Data
Collins, Terry.
    Robert E. Lee : the story of the great Confederate general / by Terry Collins;
illustrated by Cristian Mallea.
       p. cm.—(Graphic library. American graphic.)
    Includes bibliographical references and index.
    Summary: "In graphic novel format, presents Lee's surrender to Grant at the end of the
Civil War, as he recalls some of the war's most significant battles"—Provided by publisher.
       ISBN 978-1-4296-5475-3 (library binding)
       ISBN 978-1-4296-6269-7 (paperback)
       1. Lee, Robert E. (Robert Edward), 1807–1870—Juvenile literature. 2. United
States—History—Civil War, 1861–1865—Campaigns—Juvenile literature. 3. Generals—
United States—Biography—Juvenile literature. 4. Confederate States of America. Army—
Biography—Juvenile literature. 5. Graphic novels. I. Mallea, Cristian, ill. II. Title.
E467.1.L4C63 2011
973.7'3092—dc22
    [B]   2010032202

Printed in the United States of America in Stevens Point, Wisconsin.
092010   005934WZS11

TABLE of CONTENTS

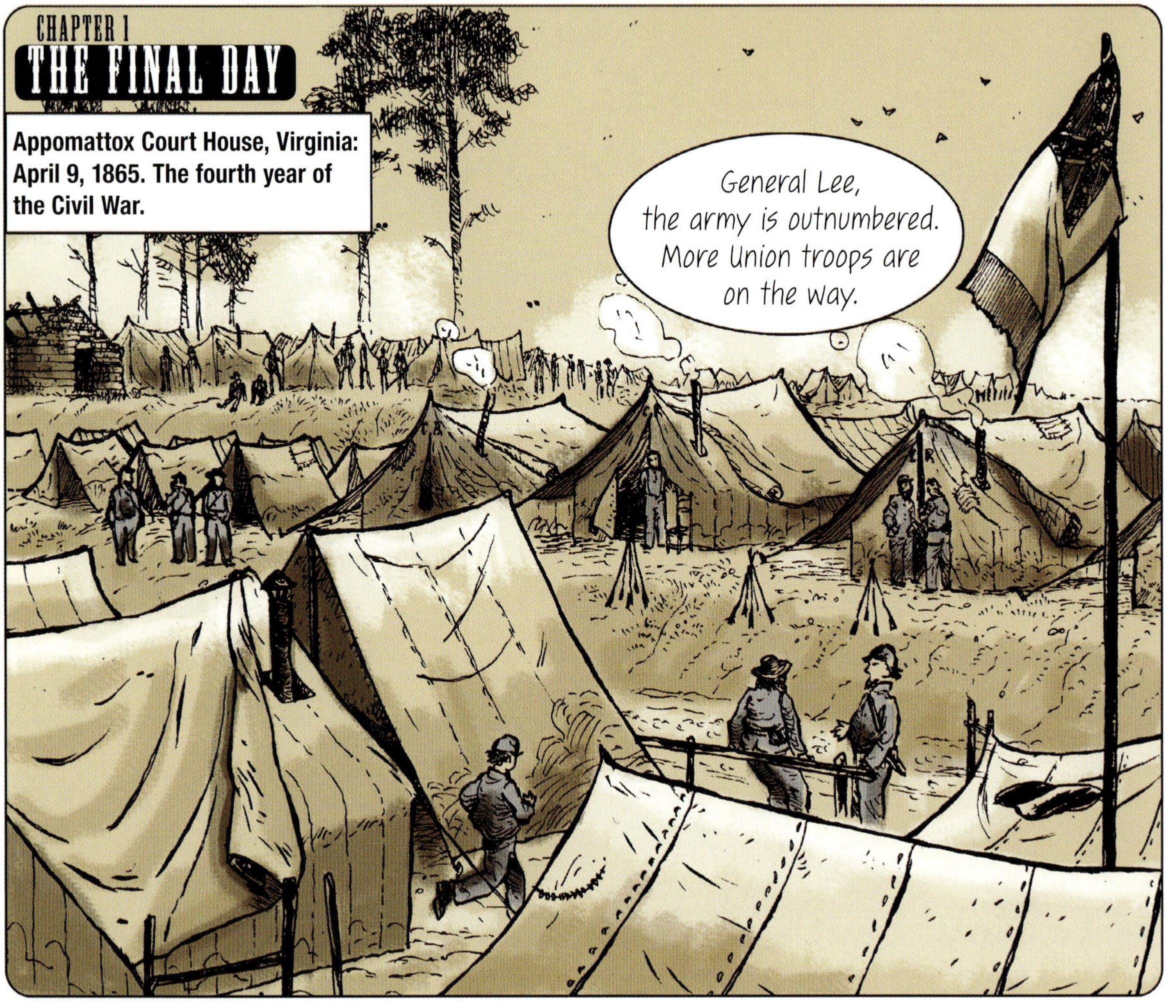
CHAPTER 1
THE FINAL DAY
Appomattox Court House, Virginia: April 9, 1865. The fourth year of the Civil War.
General Lee, the army is outnumbered. More Union troops are on the way.

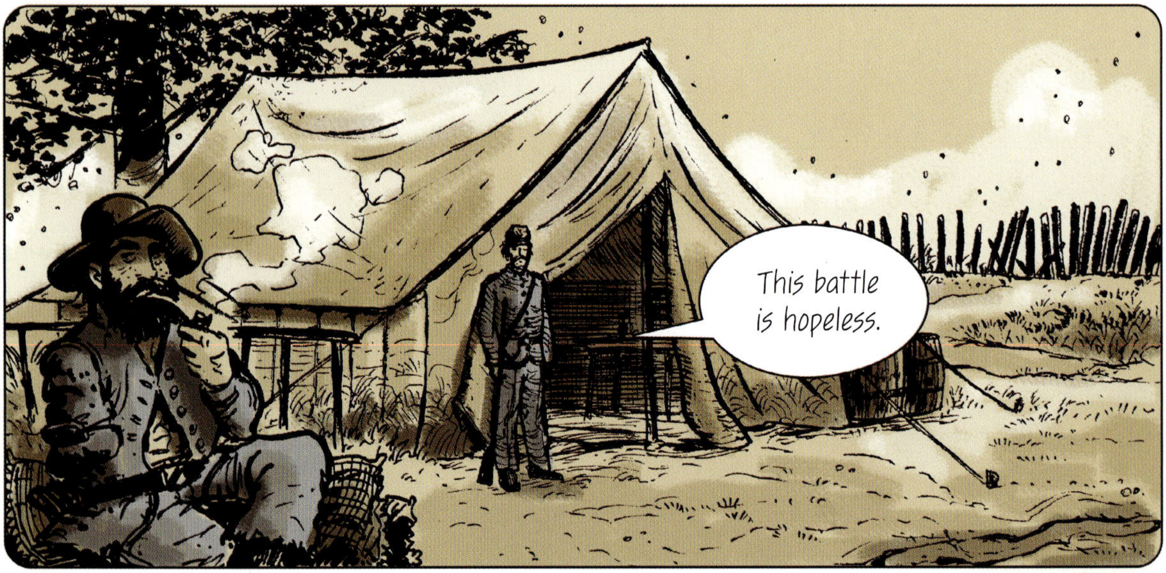
This battle is hopeless.

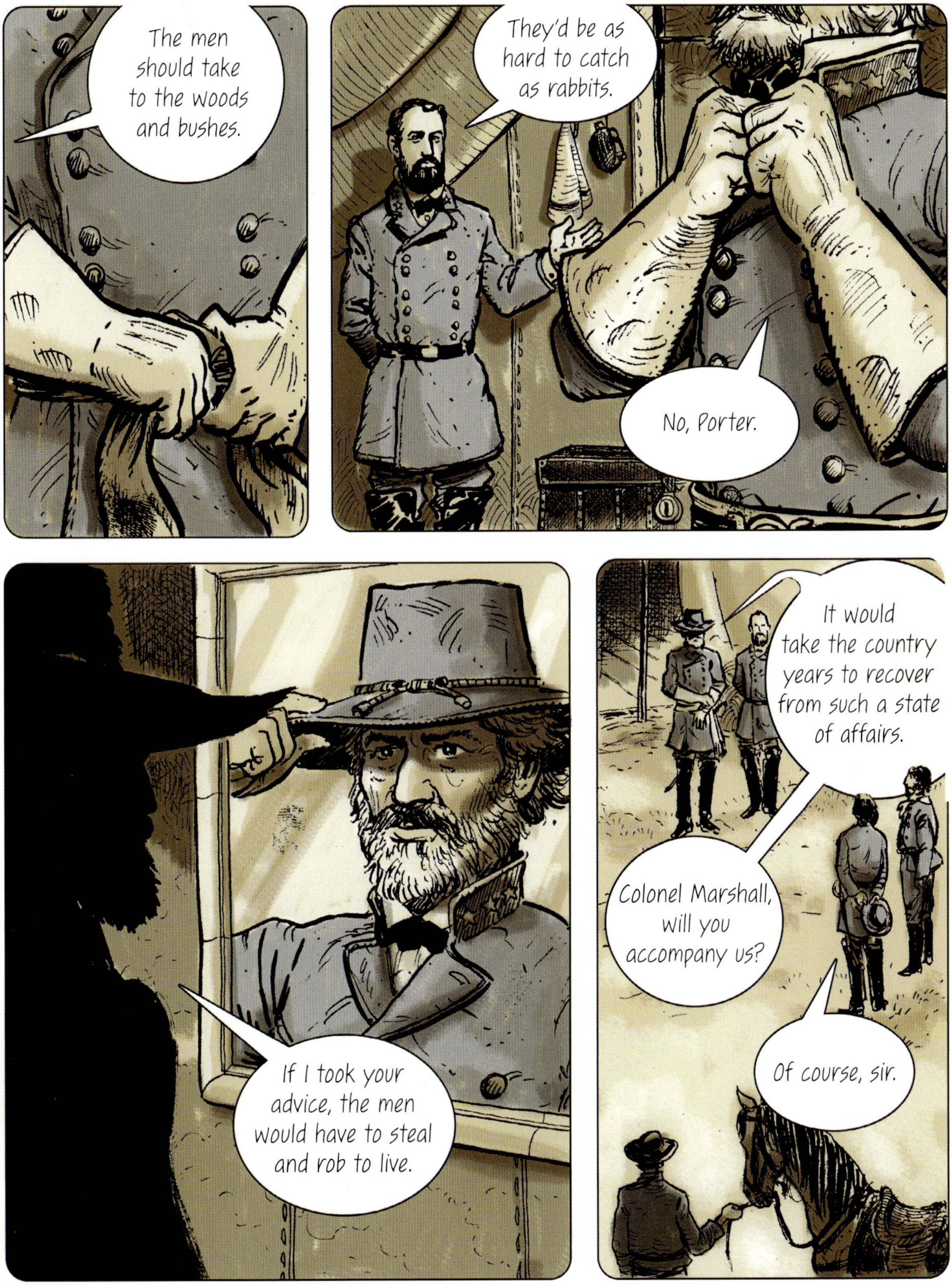
The men should take to the woods and bushes.
They'd be as hard to catch as rabbits.
No, Porter.
If I took your advice, the men would have to steal and rob to live.
It would take the country years to recover from such a state of affairs.
Colonel Marshall, will you accompany us?
Of course, sir.

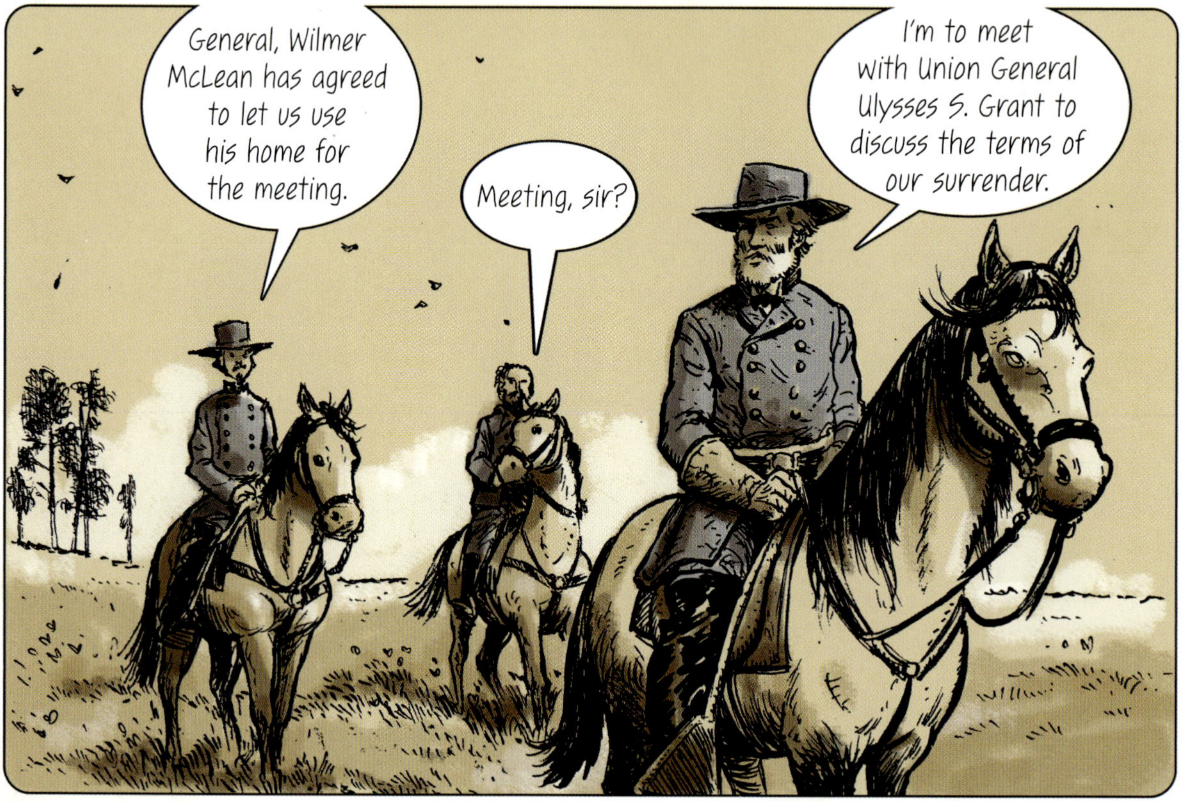
General, Wilmer McLean has agreed to let us use his home for the meeting.
Meeting, sir?
I'm to meet with Union General Ulysses S. Grant to discuss the terms of our surrender.

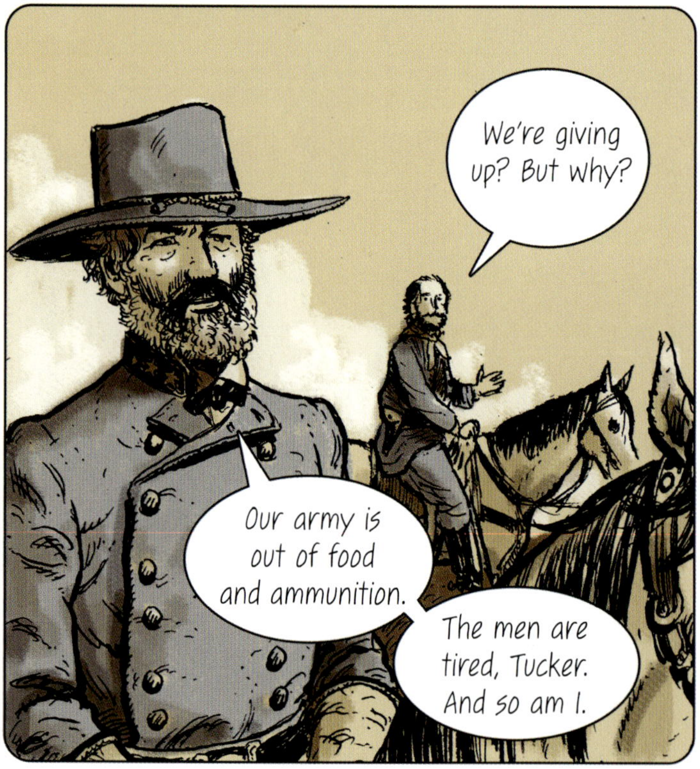
We're giving up? But why?
Our army is out of food and ammunition.
The men are tired, Tucker. And so am I.

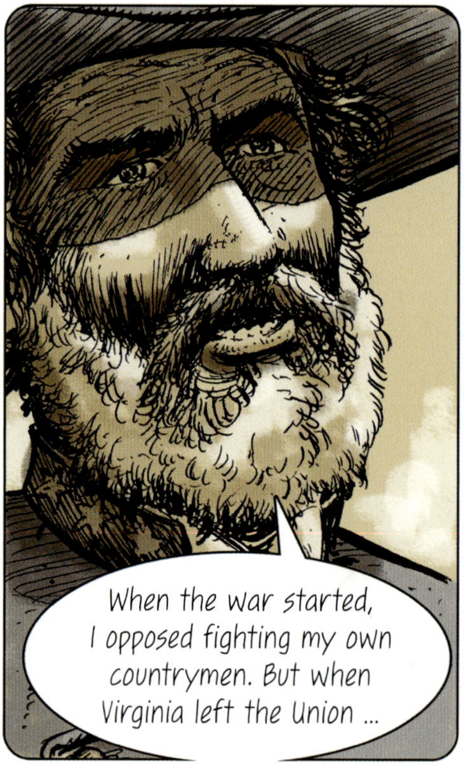
When the war started, I opposed fighting my own countrymen. But when Virginia left the Union ...

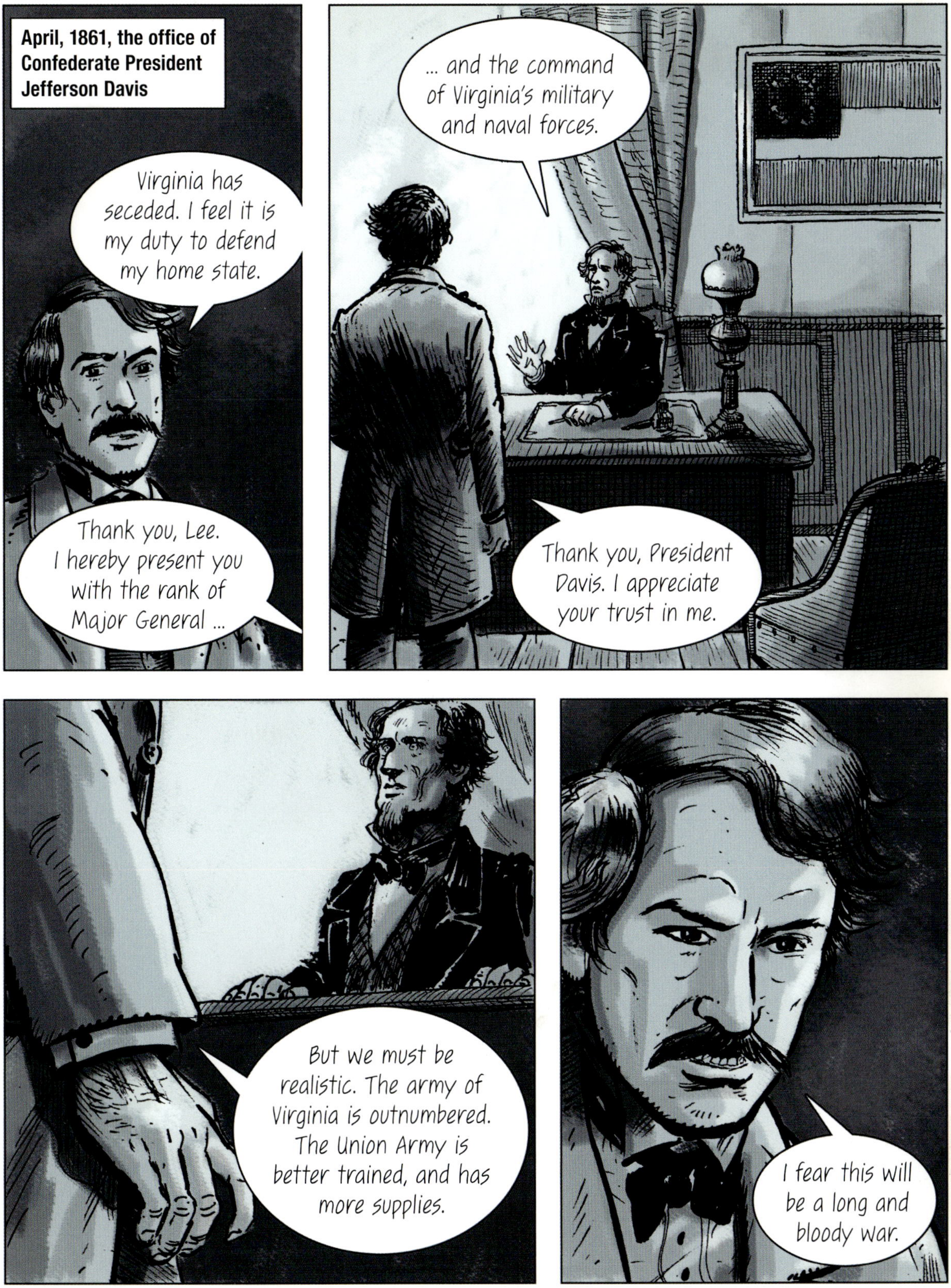
April, 1861, the office of Confederate President Jefferson Davis
Virginia has seceded. I feel it is my duty to defend my home state.
Thank you, Lee. I hereby present you with the rank of Major General ...
... and the command of Virginia's military and naval forces.
Thank you, President Davis. I appreciate your trust in me.
But we must be realistic. The army of Virginia is outnumbered. The Union Army is better trained, and has more supplies.
I fear this will be a long and bloody war.

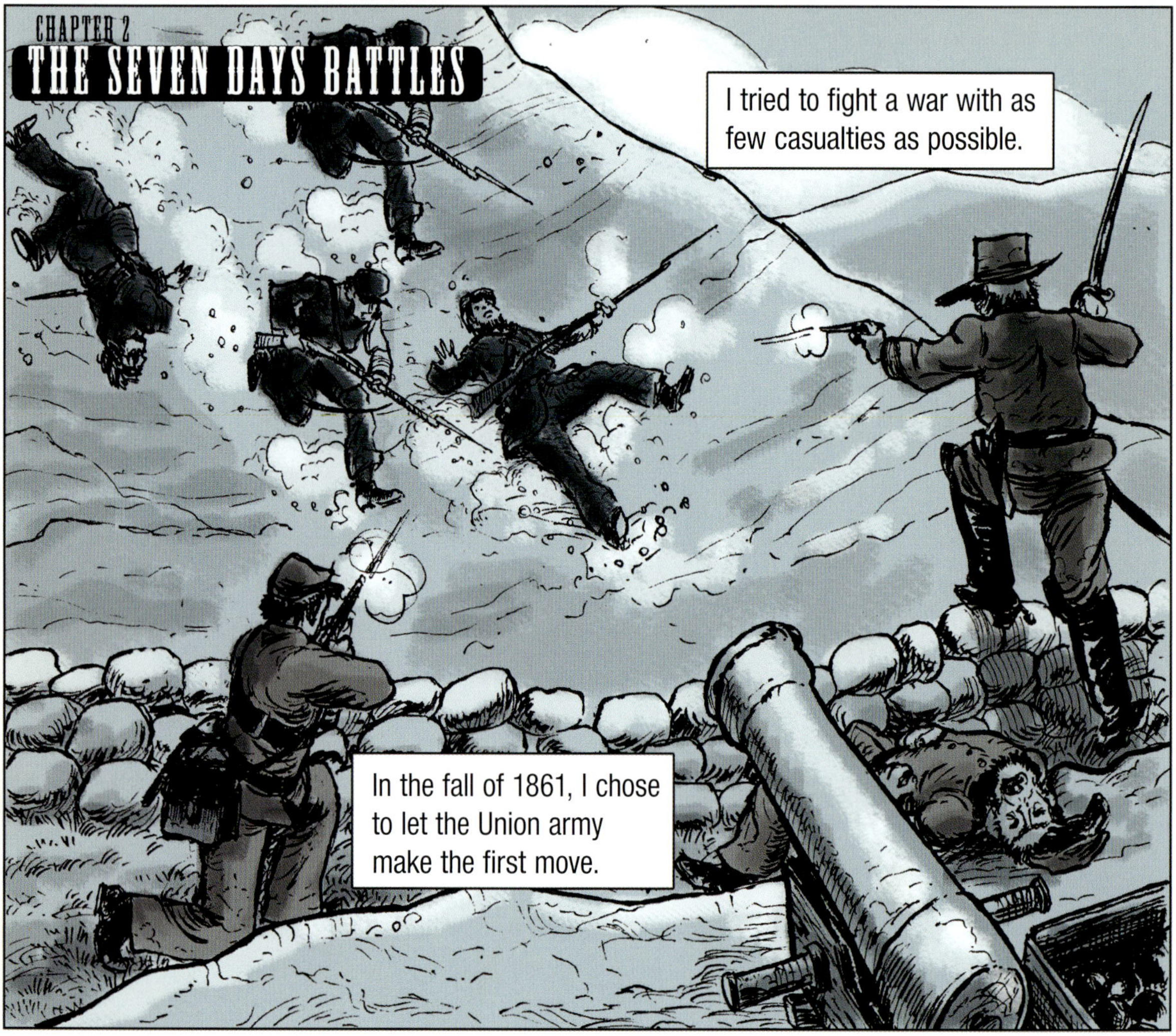
CHAPTER 2
THE SEVEN DAYS BATTLES
I tried to fight a war with as few casualties as possible.
In the fall of 1861, I chose to let the Union army make the first move.

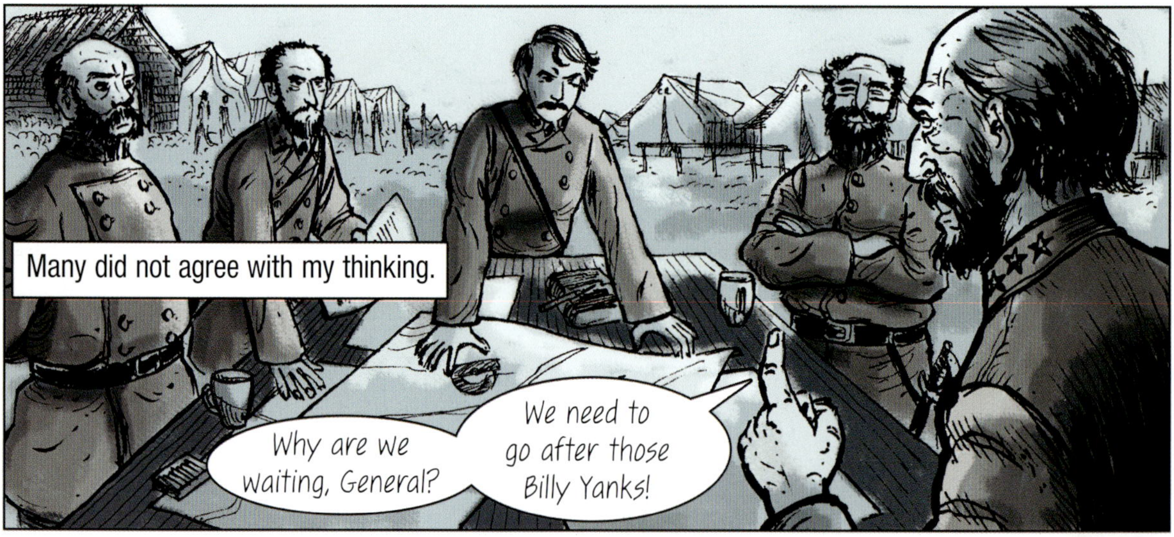
Many did not agree with my thinking.
Why are we waiting, General?
We need to go after those Billy Yanks!

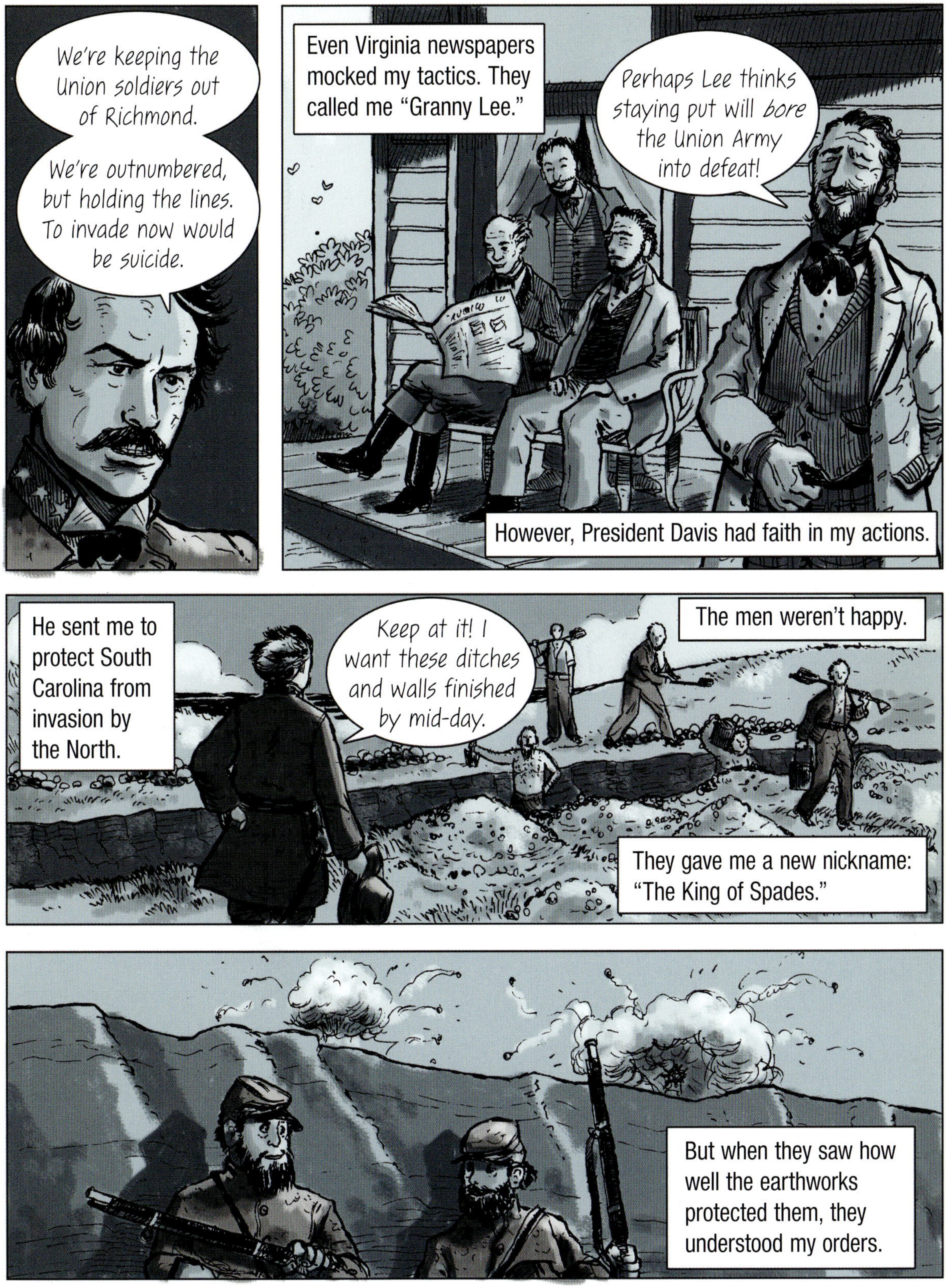
We're keeping the Union soldiers out of Richmond.
We're outnumbered, but holding the lines. To invade now would be suicide.
Even Virginia newspapers mocked my tactics. They called me "Granny Lee."
Perhaps Lee thinks staying put will *bore* the Union Army into defeat!
However, President Davis had faith in my actions.
He sent me to protect South Carolina from invasion by the North.
Keep at it! I want these ditches and walls finished by mid-day.
The men weren't happy.
They gave me a new nickname: "The King of Spades."
But when they saw how well the earthworks protected them, they understood my orders.

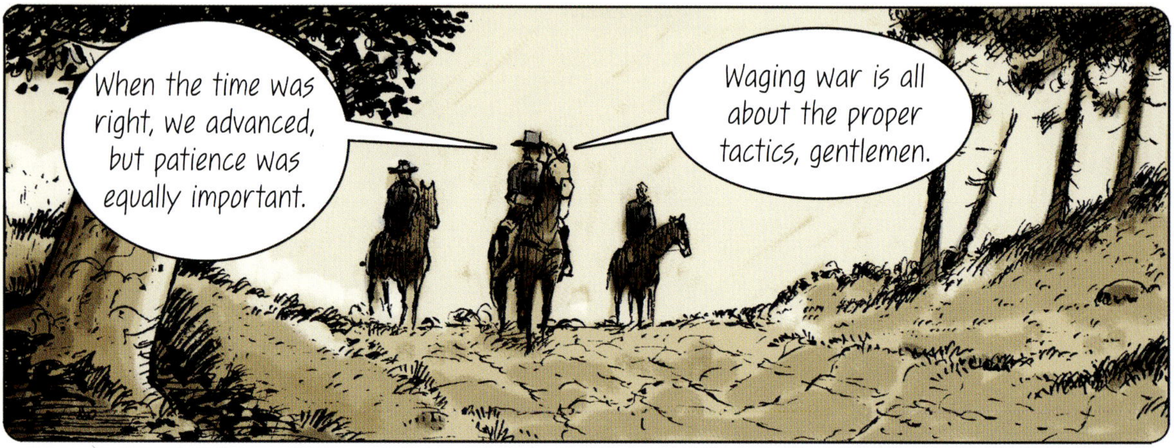
When the time was right, we advanced, but patience was equally important.
Waging war is all about the proper tactics, gentlemen.

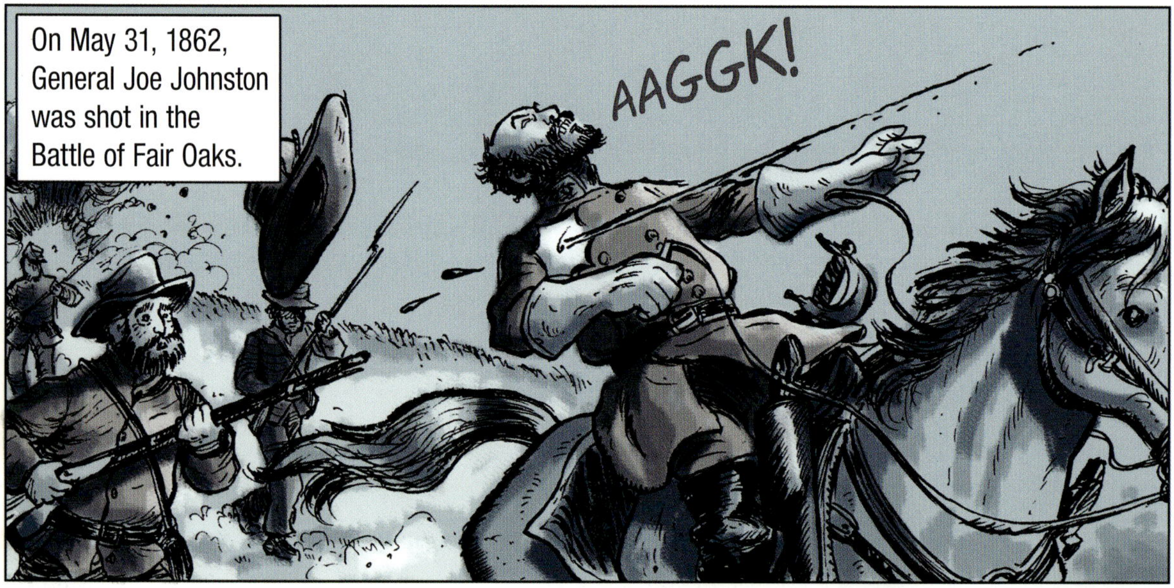
On May 31, 1862, General Joe Johnston was shot in the Battle of Fair Oaks.
AAGGK!

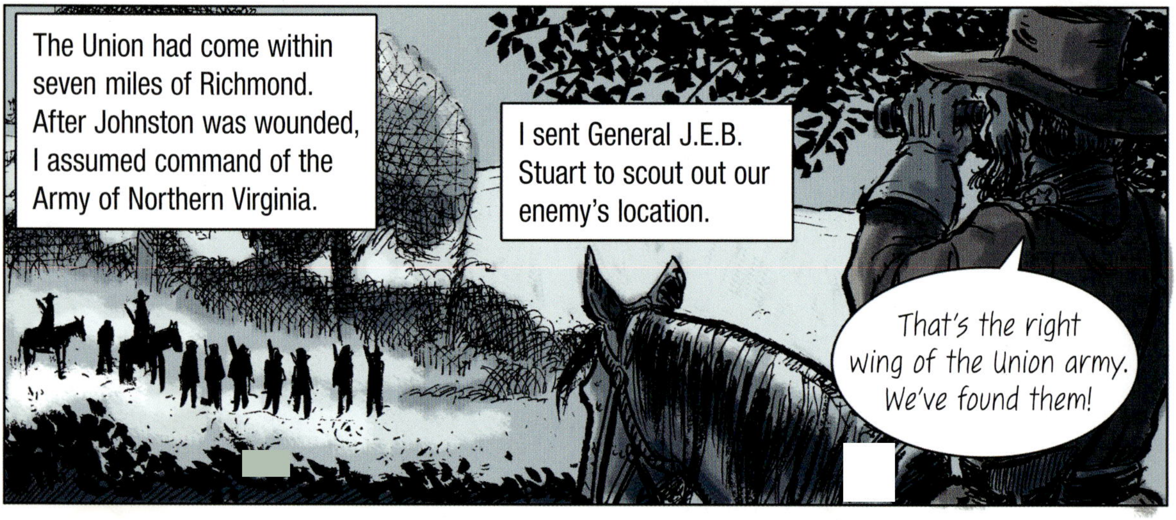
The Union had come within seven miles of Richmond. After Johnston was wounded, I assumed command of the Army of Northern Virginia.
I sent General J.E.B. Stuart to scout out our enemy's location.
That's the right wing of the Union army. We've found them!

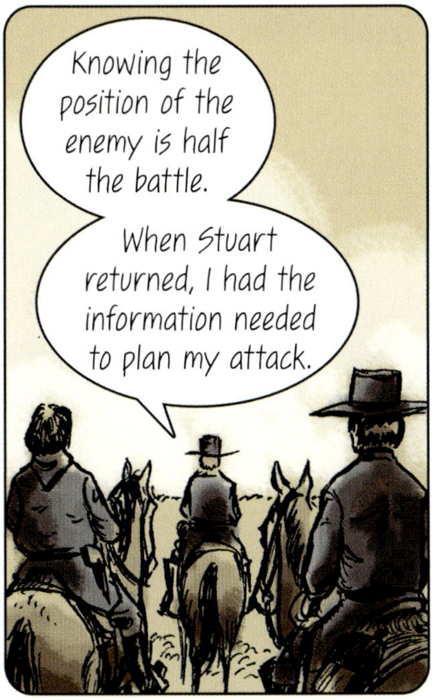
Knowing the position of the enemy is half the battle.
When Stuart returned, I had the information needed to plan my attack.

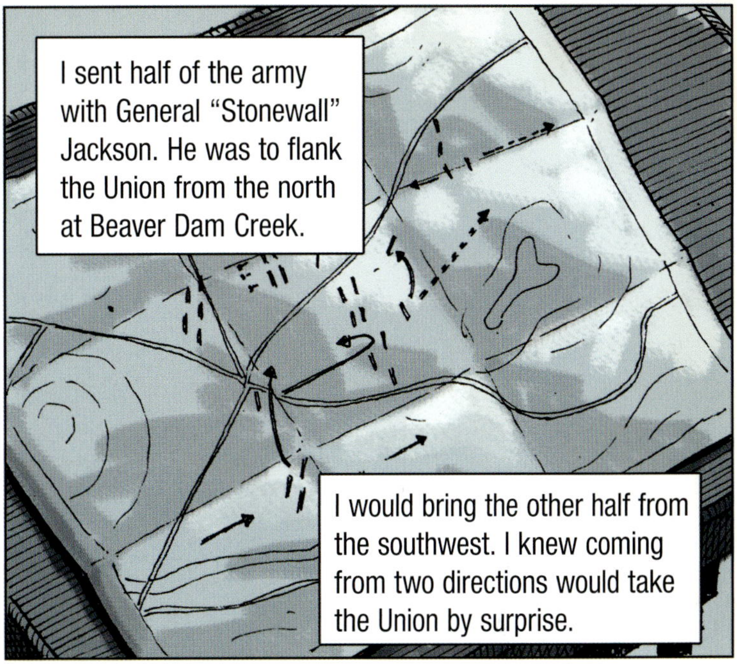
I sent half of the army with General "Stonewall" Jackson. He was to flank the Union from the north at Beaver Dam Creek.
I would bring the other half from the southwest. I knew coming from two directions would take the Union by surprise.

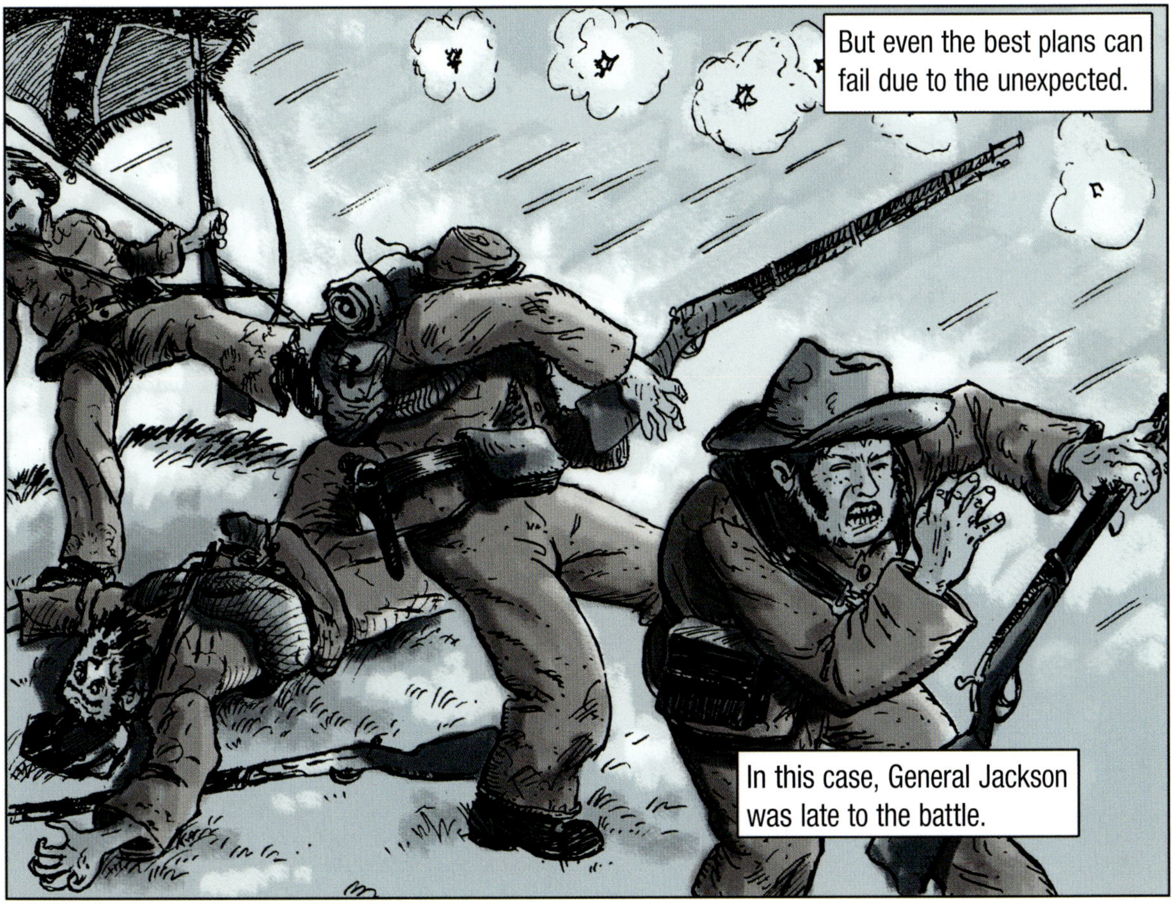
But even the best plans can fail due to the unexpected.
In this case, General Jackson was late to the battle.

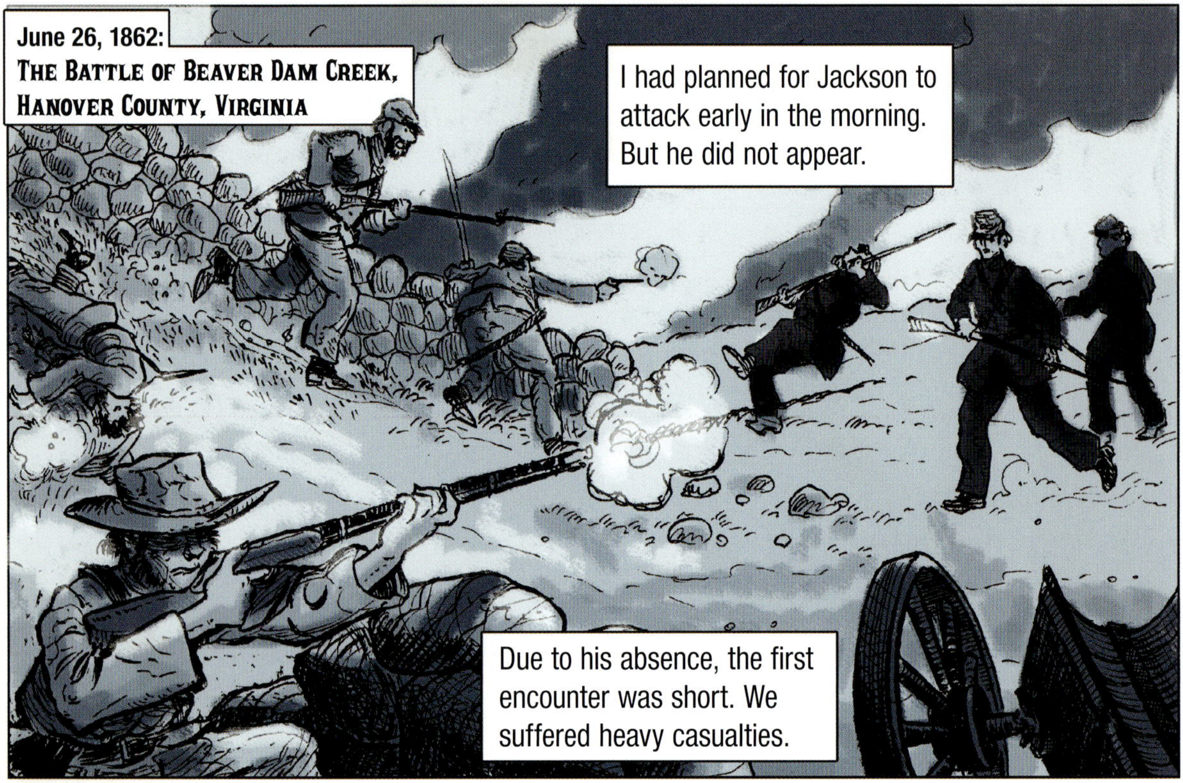
June 26, 1862:
THE BATTLE OF BEAVER DAM CREEK, HANOVER COUNTY, VIRGINIA
I had planned for Jackson to attack early in the morning. But he did not appear.
Due to his absence, the first encounter was short. We suffered heavy casualties.

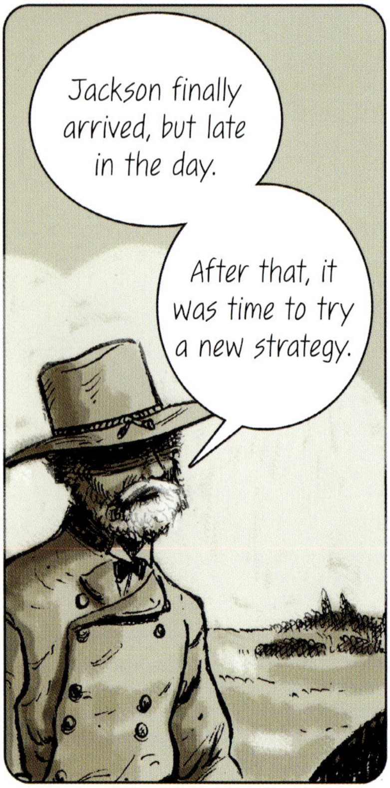
Jackson finally arrived, but late in the day.
After that, it was time to try a new strategy.

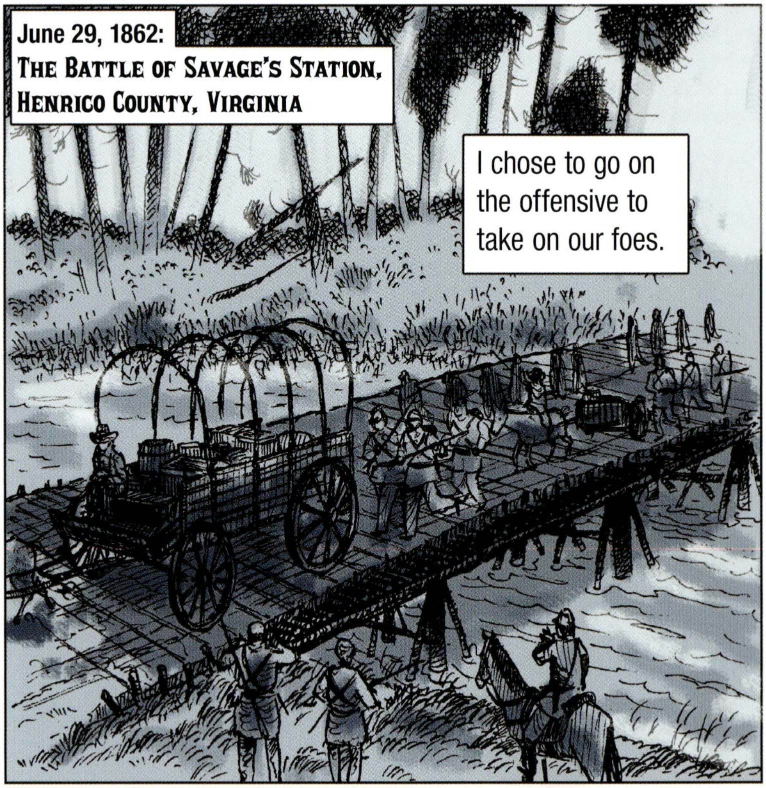
June 29, 1862:
THE BATTLE OF SAVAGE'S STATION, HENRICO COUNTY, VIRGINIA
I chose to go on the offensive to take on our foes.

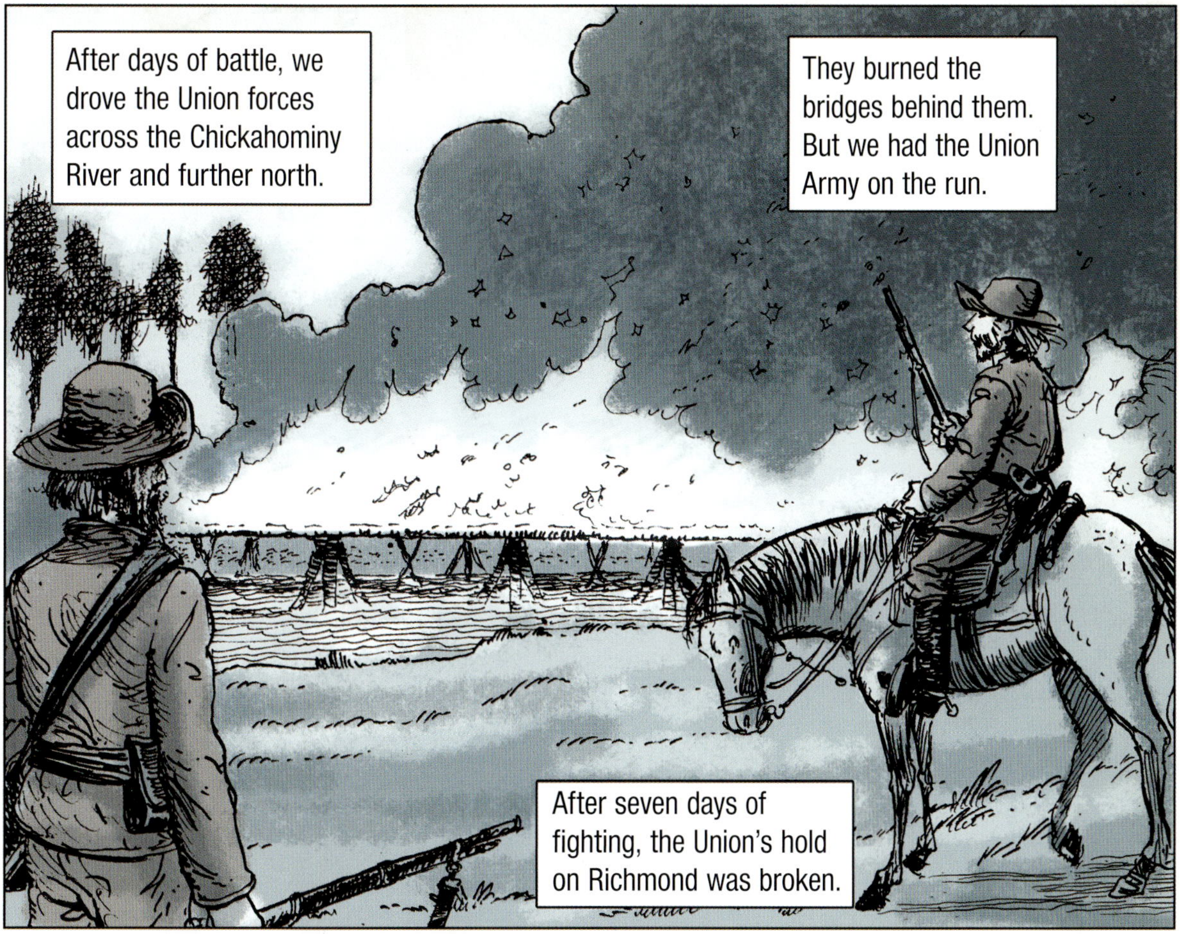
After days of battle, we drove the Union forces across the Chickahominy River and further north.
They burned the bridges behind them. But we had the Union Army on the run.
After seven days of fighting, the Union's hold on Richmond was broken.

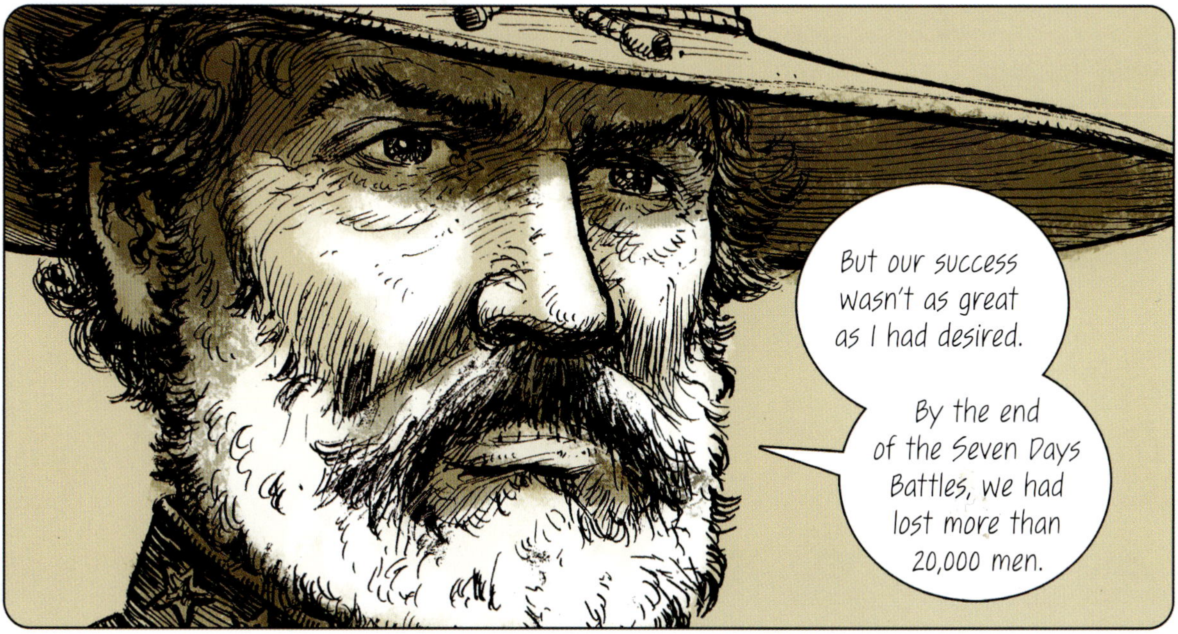
But our success wasn't as great as I had desired.
By the end of the Seven Days Battles, we had lost more than 20,000 men.

CHAPTER 3
THE BATTLE OF ANTIETAM

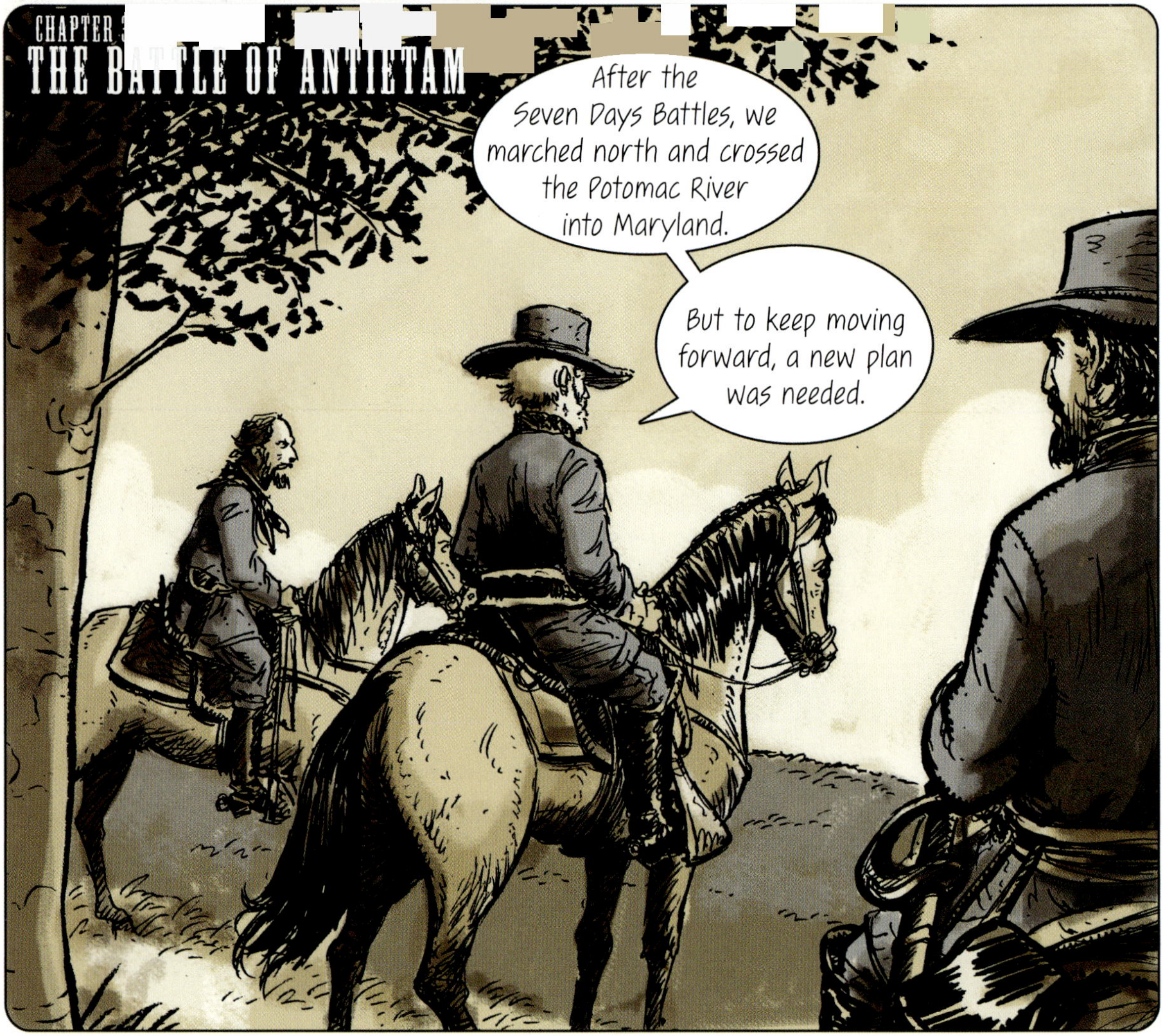

After the Seven Days Battles, we marched north and crossed the Potomac River into Maryland.
But to keep moving forward, a new plan was needed.

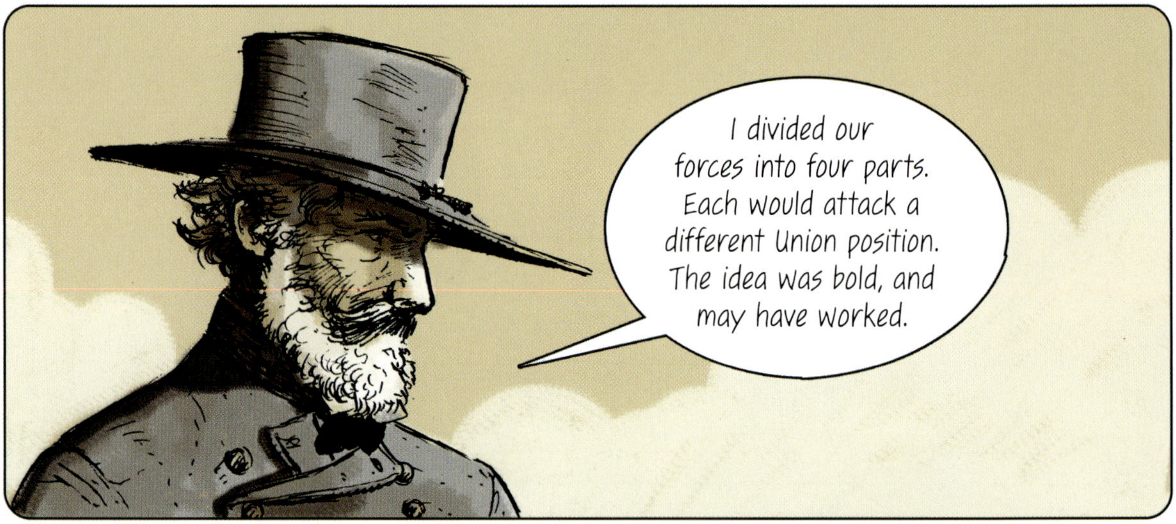

I divided our forces into four parts. Each would attack a different Union position. The idea was bold, and may have worked.

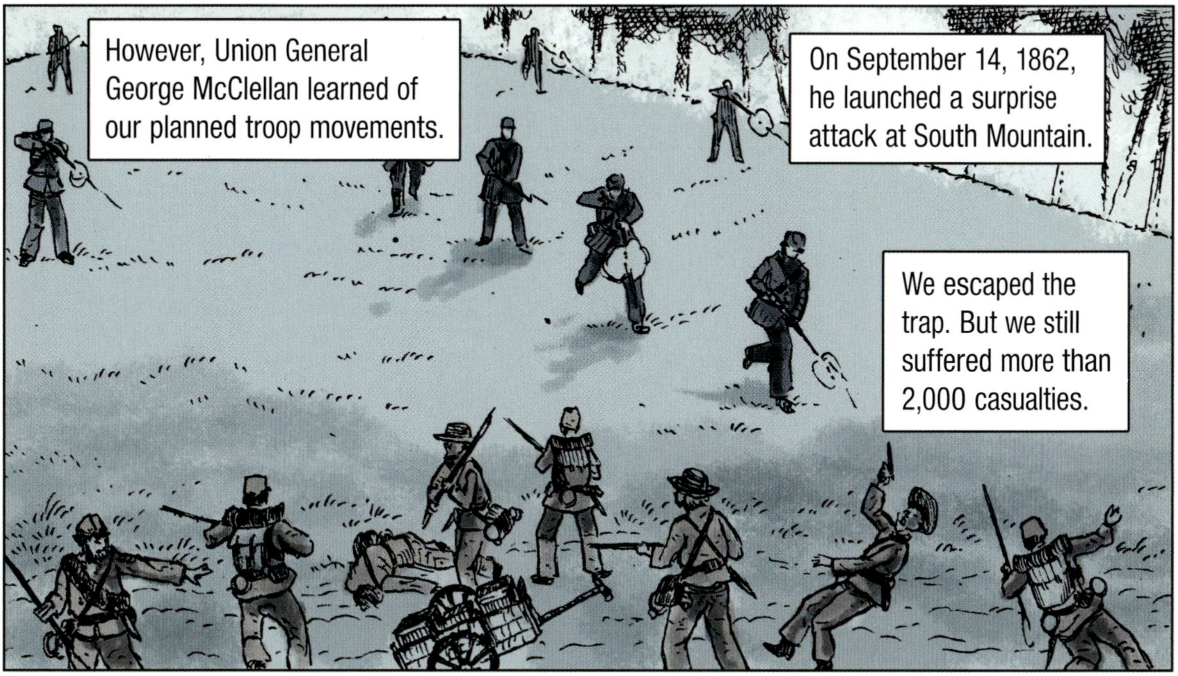

However, Union General George McClellan learned of our planned troop movements.
On September 14, 1862, he launched a surprise attack at South Mountain.
We escaped the trap. But we still suffered more than 2,000 casualties.

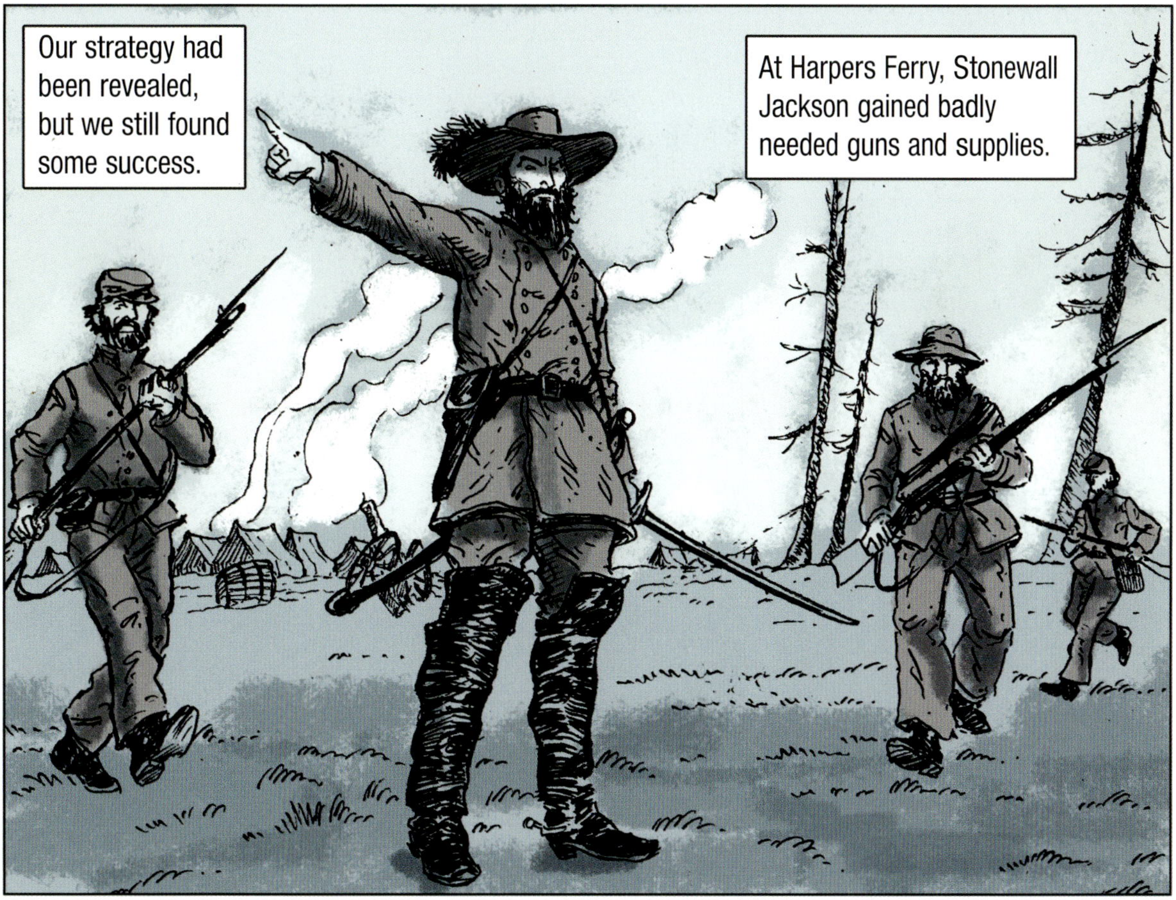

Our strategy had been revealed, but we still found some success.
At Harpers Ferry, Stonewall Jackson gained badly needed guns and supplies.

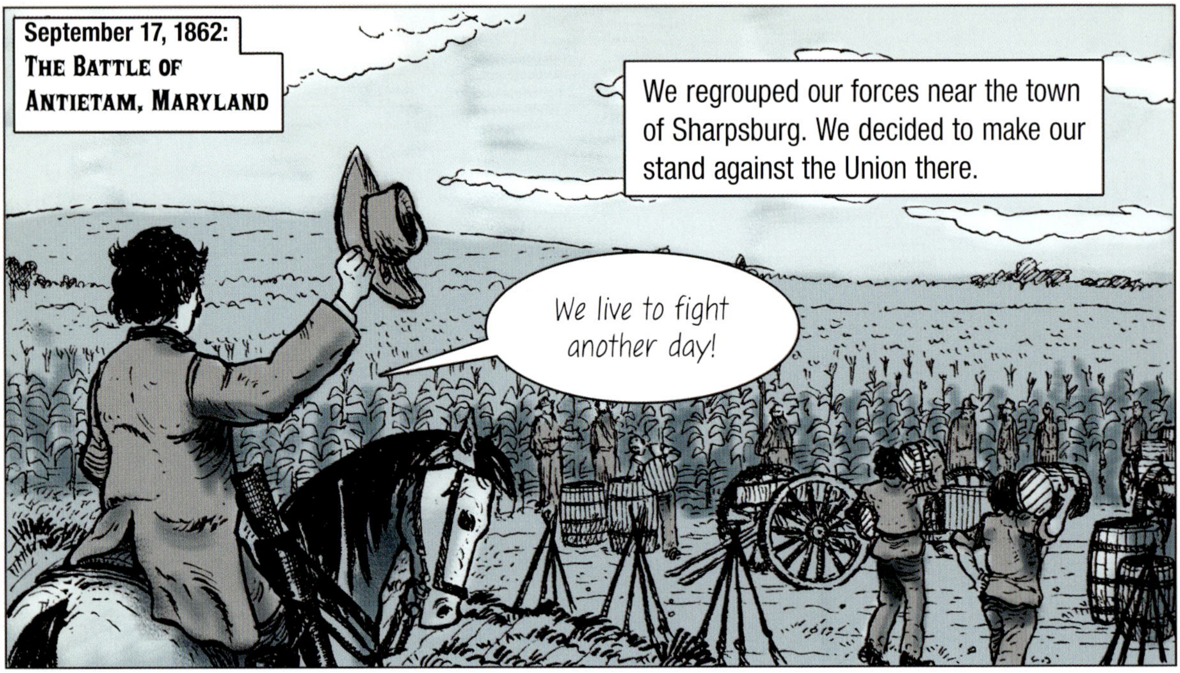
September 17, 1862:
The Battle of Antietam, Maryland
We regrouped our forces near the town of Sharpsburg. We decided to make our stand against the Union there.
We live to fight another day!

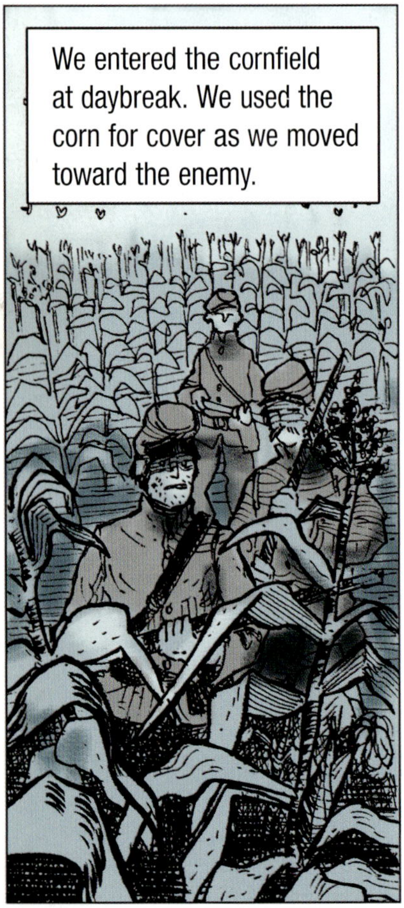
We entered the cornfield at daybreak. We used the corn for cover as we moved toward the enemy.

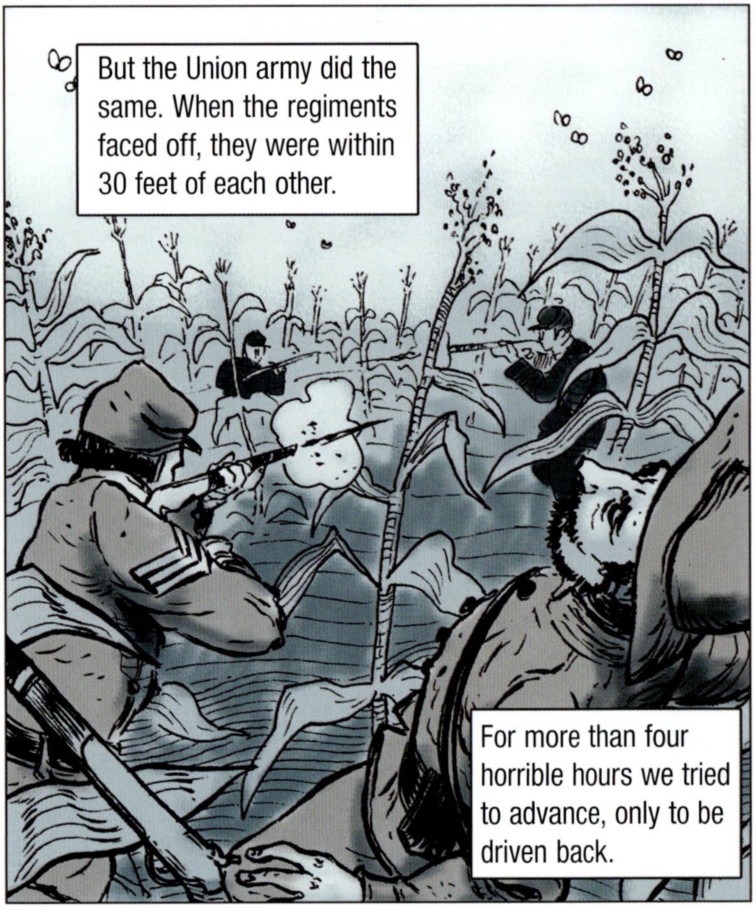
But the Union army did the same. When the regiments faced off, they were within 30 feet of each other.
For more than four horrible hours we tried to advance, only to be driven back.

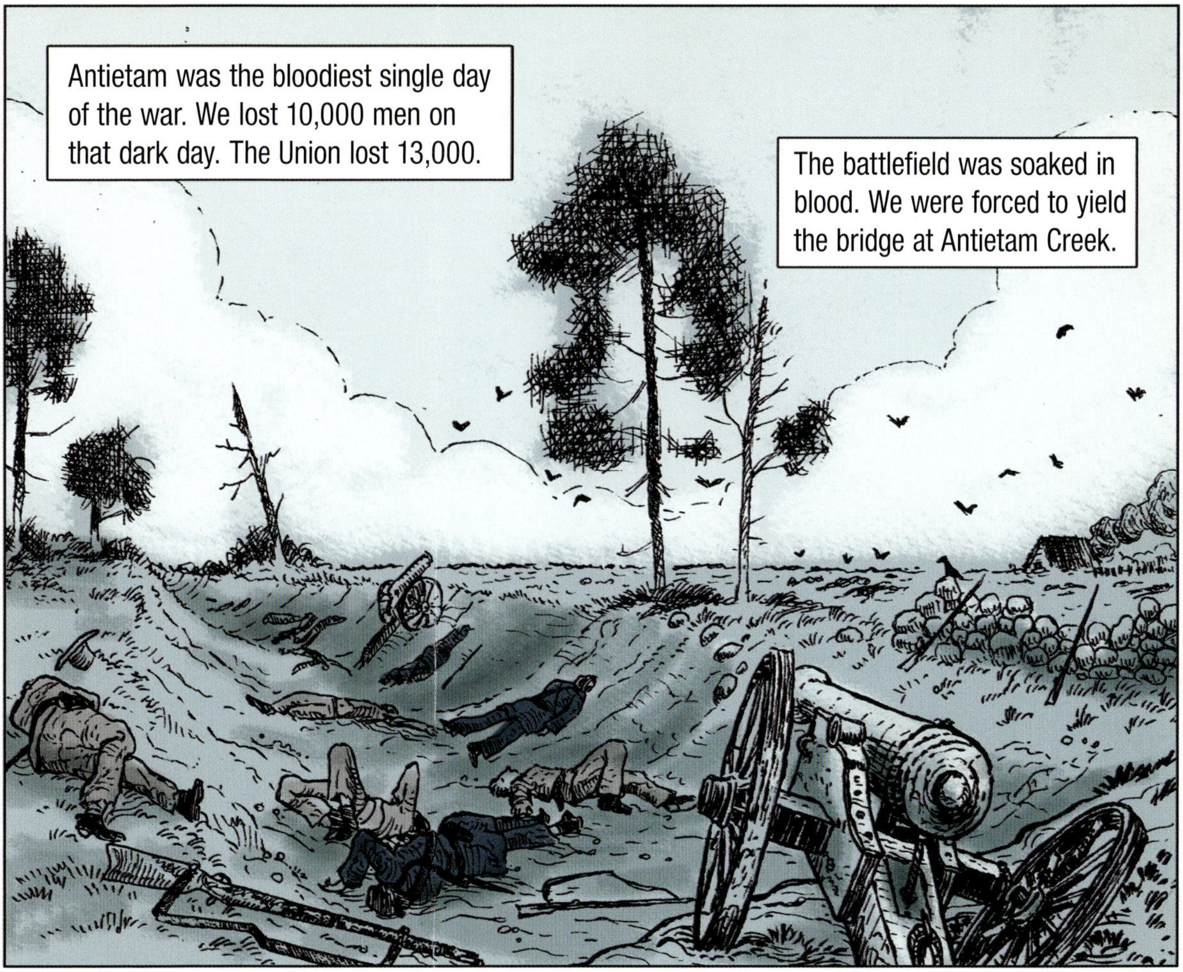
Antietam was the bloodiest single day of the war. We lost 10,000 men on that dark day. The Union lost 13,000.
The battlefield was soaked in blood. We were forced to yield the bridge at Antietam Creek.

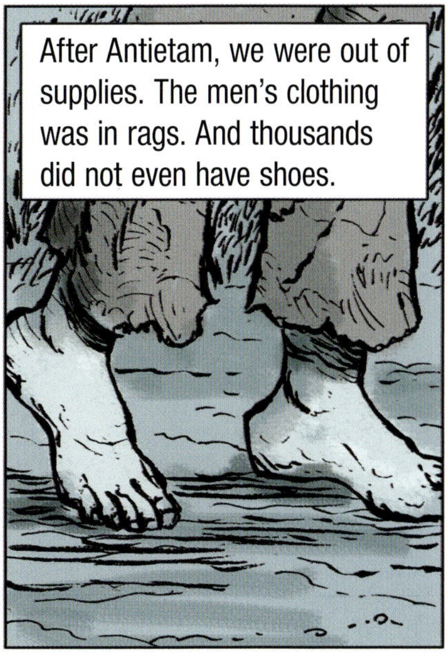
After Antietam, we were out of supplies. The men's clothing was in rags. And thousands did not even have shoes.

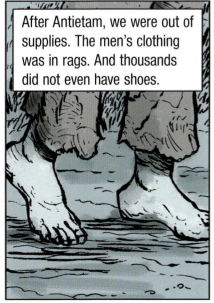

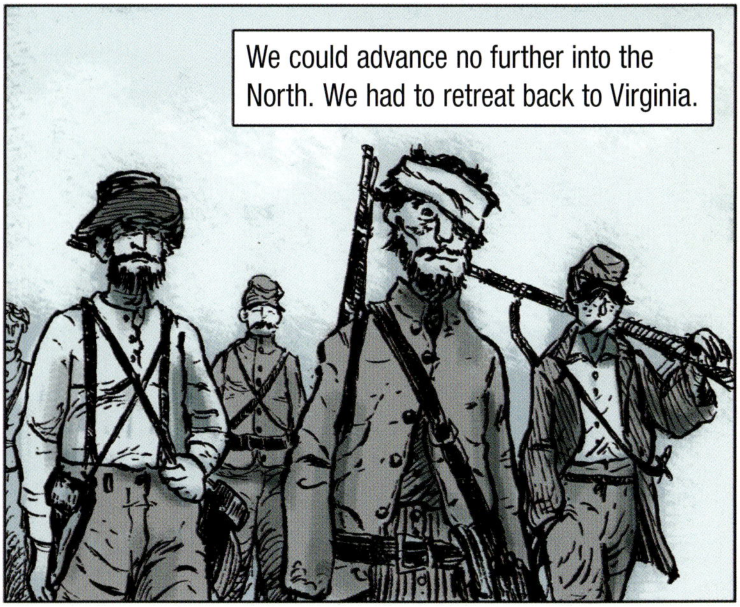
We could advance no further into the North. We had to retreat back to Virginia.

CHAPTER 4
THE BATTLE OF CHANCELLORSVILLE

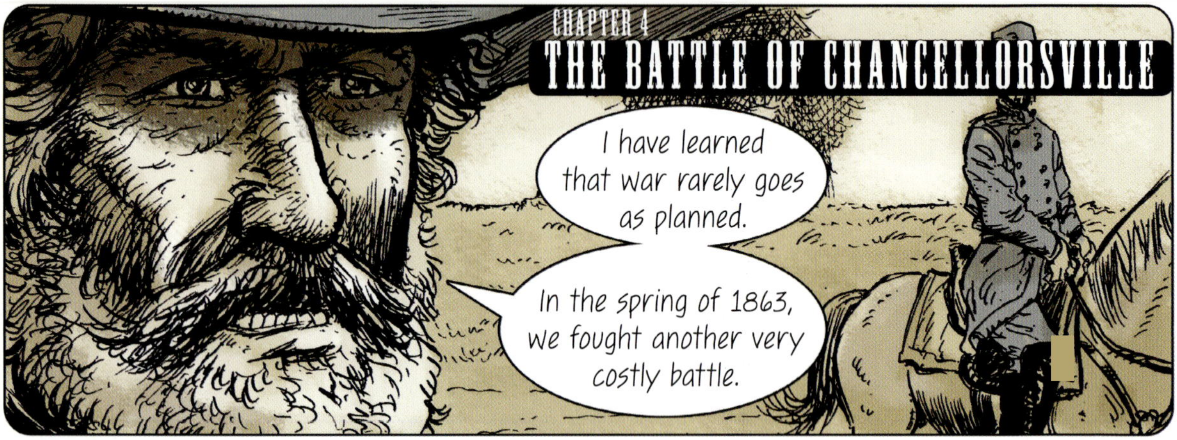
I have learned that war rarely goes as planned.
In the spring of 1863, we fought another very costly battle.

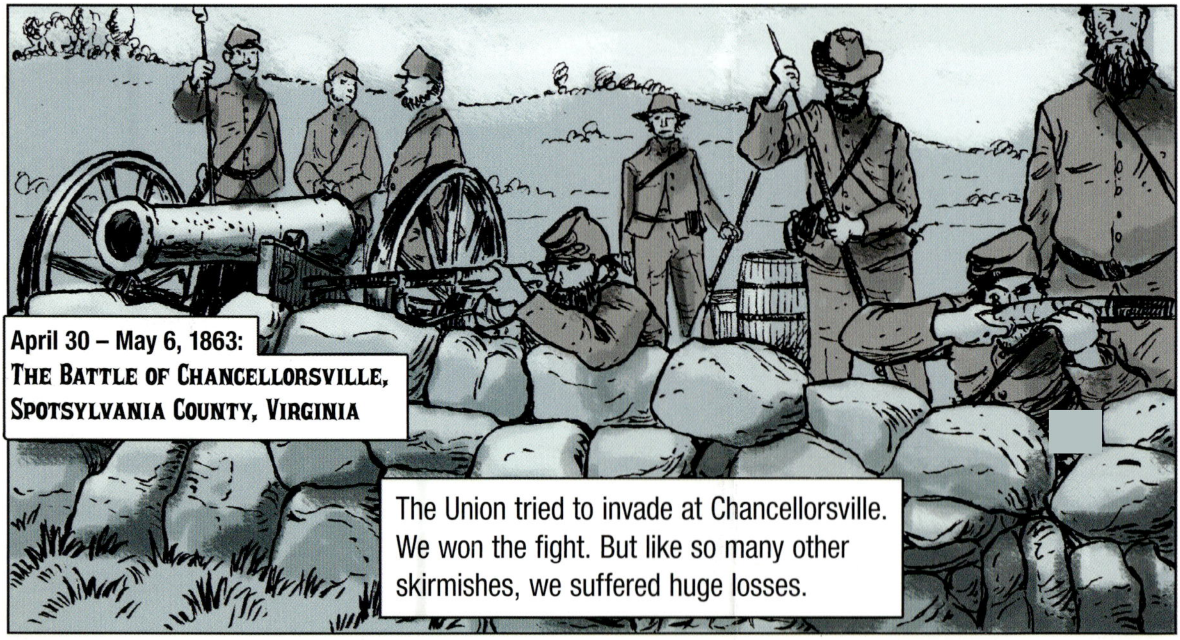
April 30 – May 6, 1863:
THE BATTLE OF CHANCELLORSVILLE, SPOTSYLVANIA COUNTY, VIRGINIA
The Union tried to invade at Chancellorsville. We won the fight. But like so many other skirmishes, we suffered huge losses.

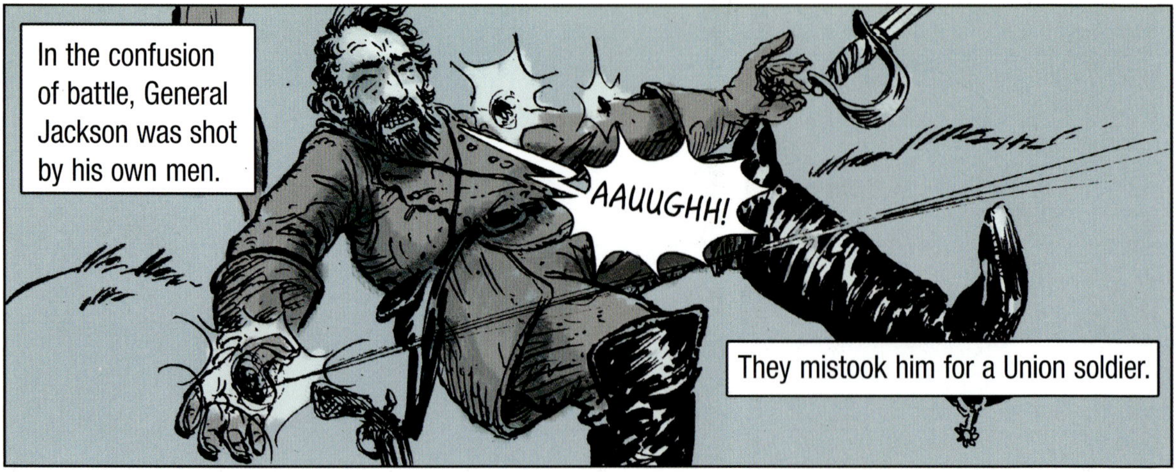
In the confusion of battle, General Jackson was shot by his own men.
AAUUGHH!
They mistook him for a Union soldier.

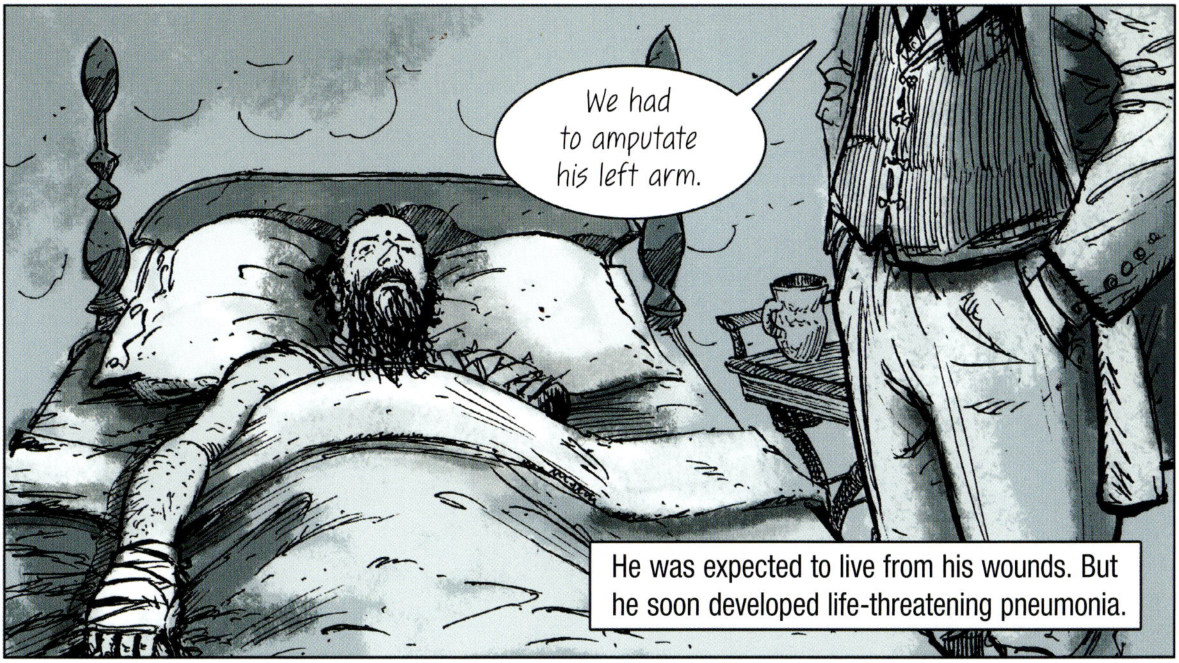
We had to amputate his left arm.
He was expected to live from his wounds. But he soon developed life-threatening pneumonia.

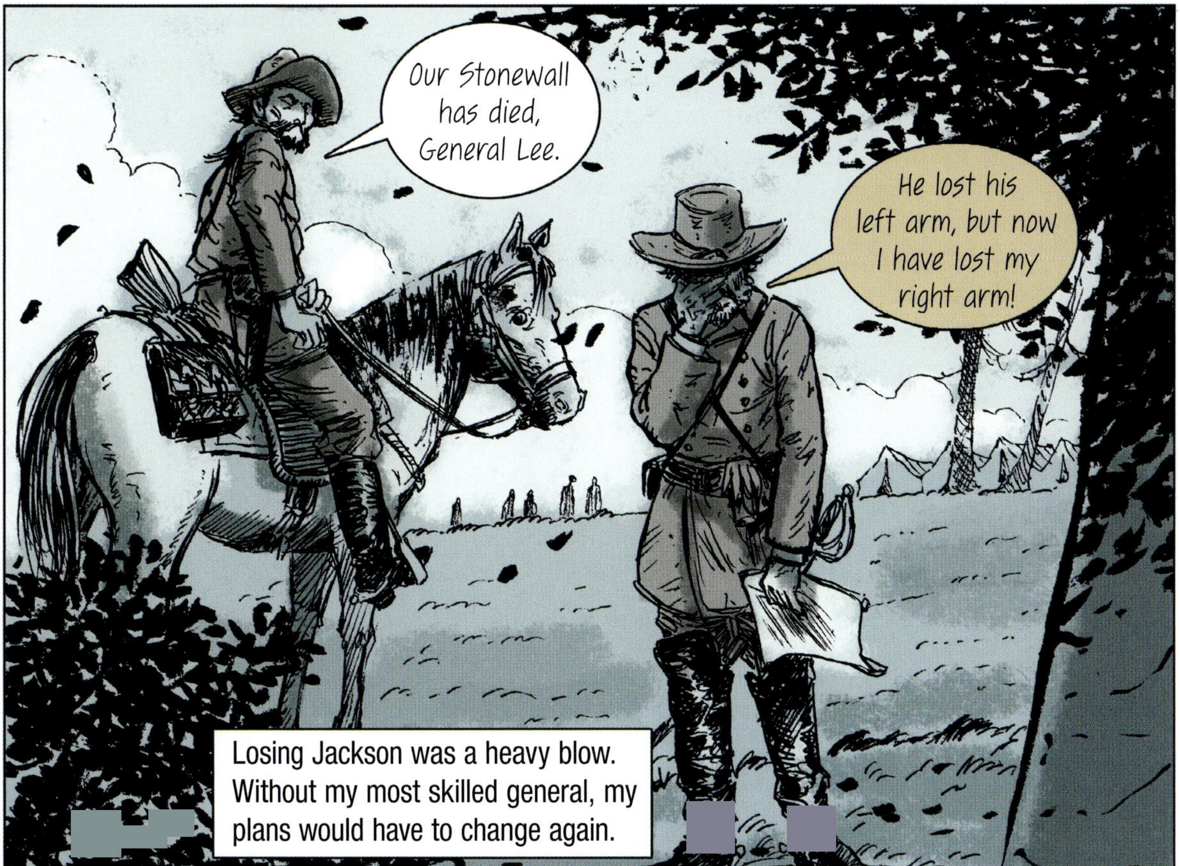
Our Stonewall has died, General Lee.
He lost his left arm, but now I have lost my right arm!
Losing Jackson was a heavy blow. Without my most skilled general, my plans would have to change again.

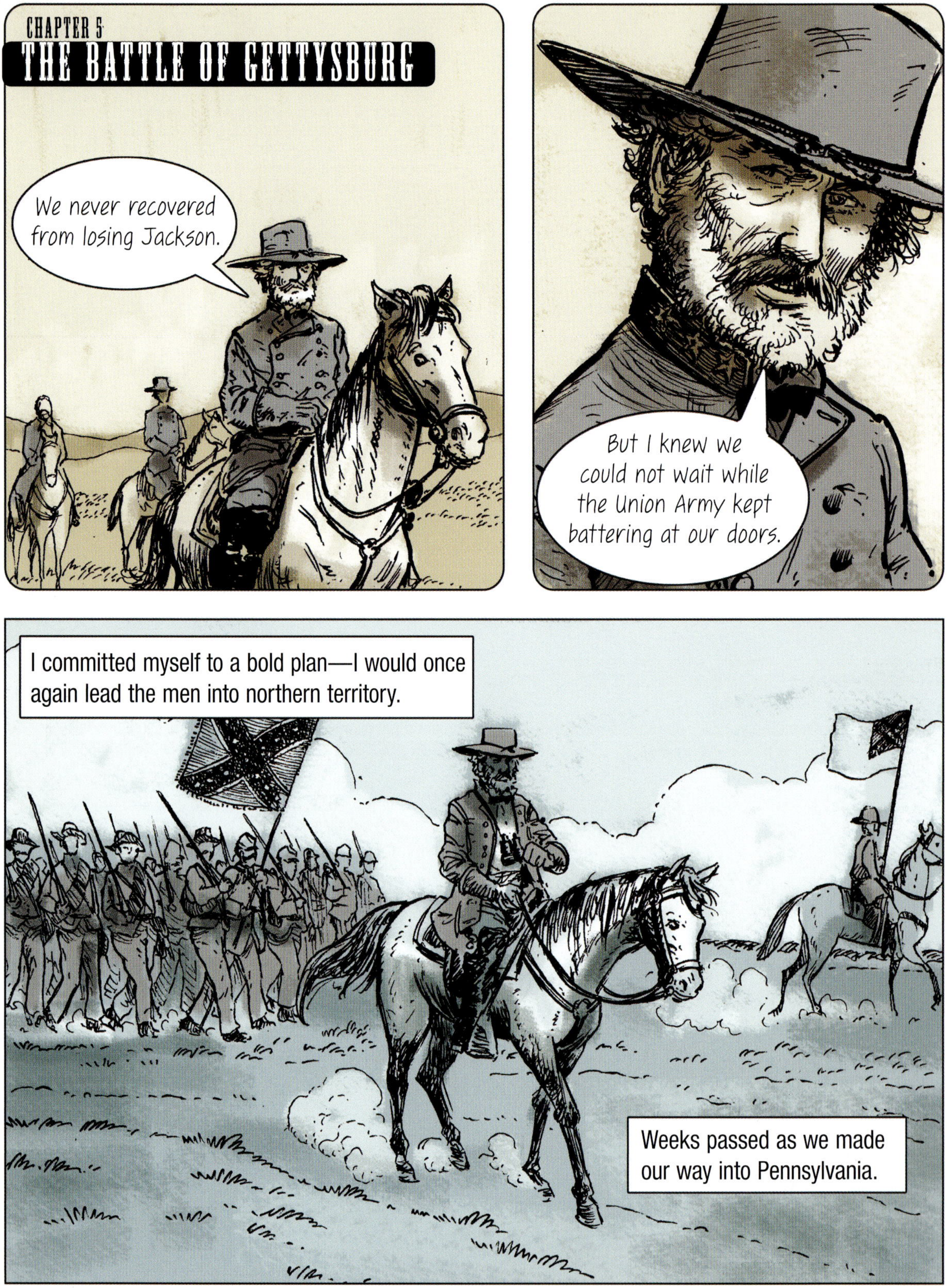
CHAPTER 5
THE BATTLE OF GETTYSBURG
We never recovered from losing Jackson.
But I knew we could not wait while the Union Army kept battering at our doors.
I committed myself to a bold plan—I would once again lead the men into northern territory.
Weeks passed as we made our way into Pennsylvania.

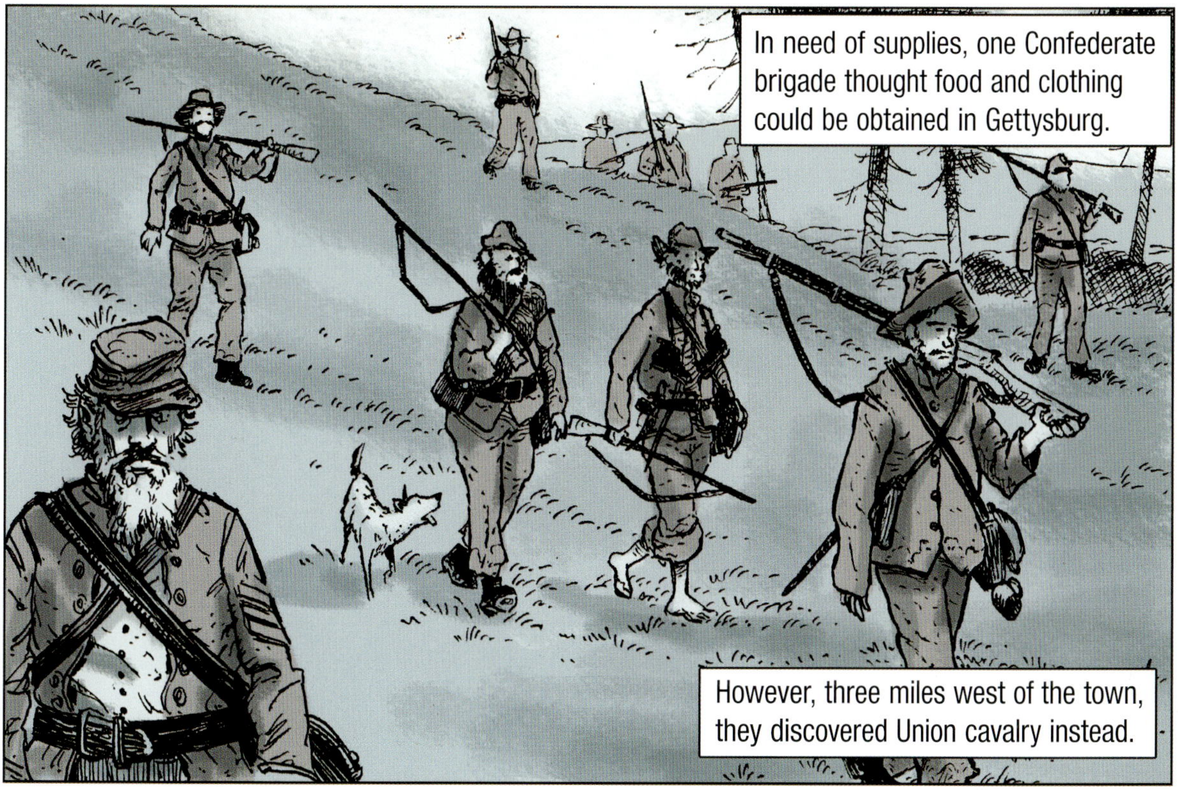
In need of supplies, one Confederate brigade thought food and clothing could be obtained in Gettysburg.
However, three miles west of the town, they discovered Union cavalry instead.

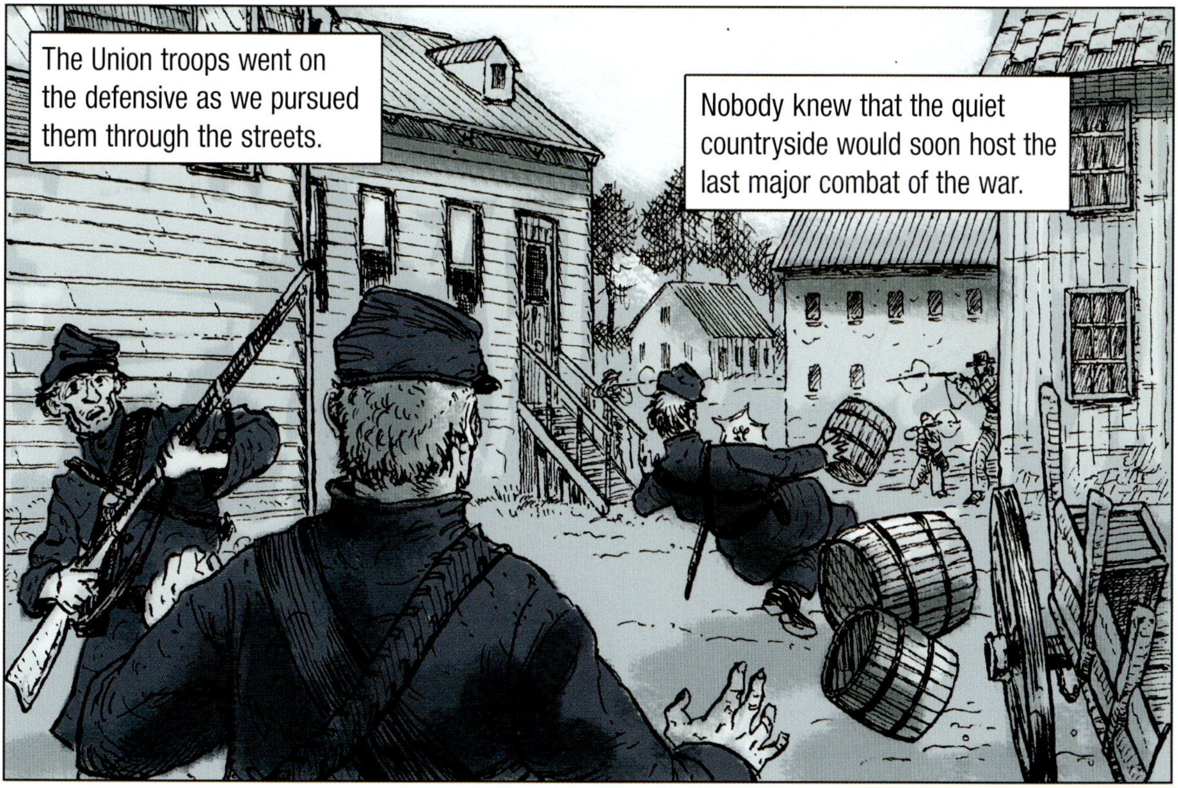
The Union troops went on the defensive as we pursued them through the streets.
Nobody knew that the quiet countryside would soon host the last major combat of the war.

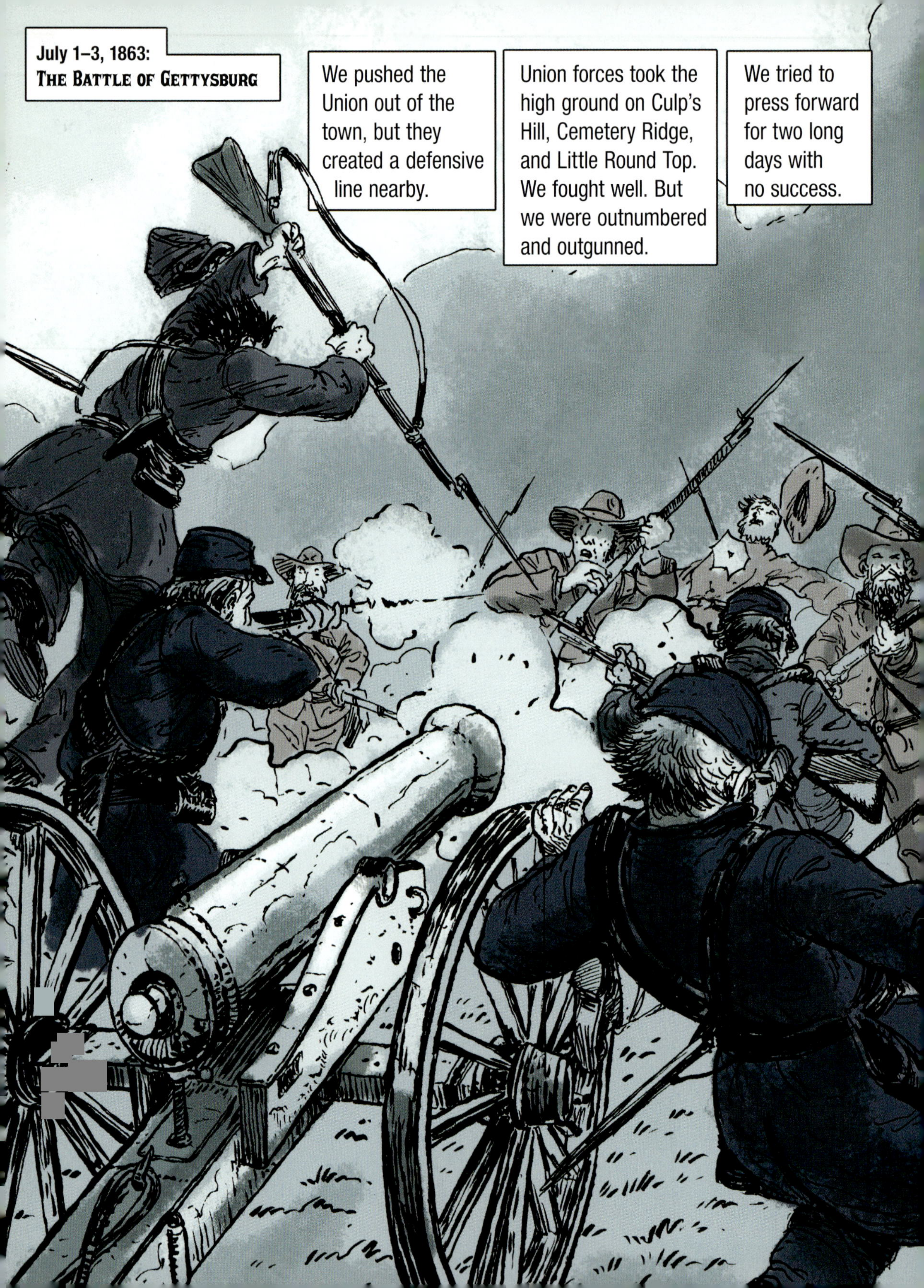
July 1–3, 1863:
THE BATTLE OF GETTYSBURG
We pushed the Union out of the town, but they created a defensive line nearby.
Union forces took the high ground on Culp's Hill, Cemetery Ridge, and Little Round Top. We fought well. But we were outnumbered and outgunned.
We tried to press forward for two long days with no success.

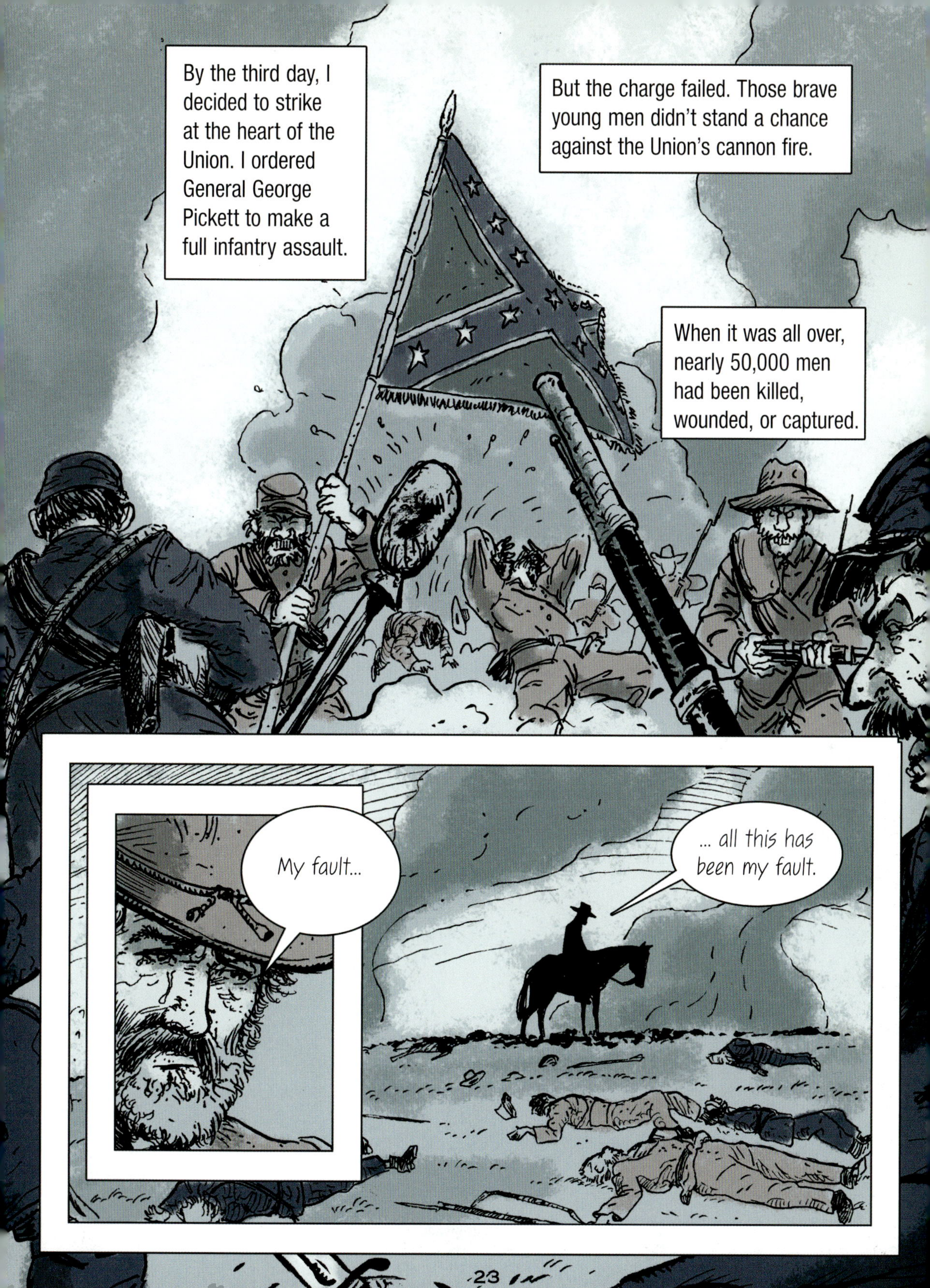
By the third day, I decided to strike at the heart of the Union. I ordered General George Pickett to make a full infantry assault.
But the charge failed. Those brave young men didn't stand a chance against the Union's cannon fire.
When it was all over, nearly 50,000 men had been killed, wounded, or captured.
My fault...
... all this has been my fault.

CHAPTER 6

SURRENDER AT APPOMATTOX

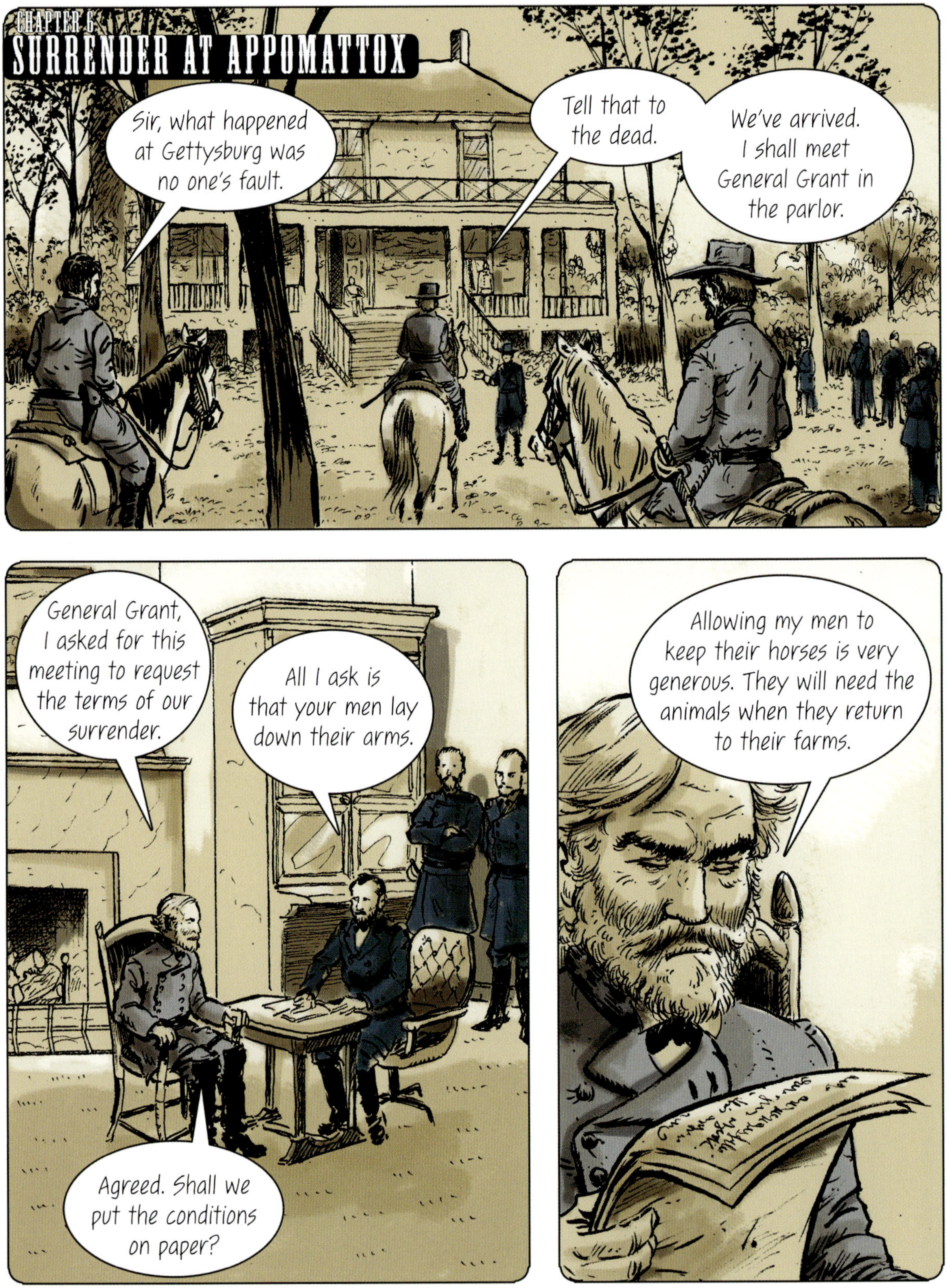
Sir, what happened at Gettysburg was no one's fault.
Tell that to the dead.
We've arrived. I shall meet General Grant in the parlor.
General Grant, I asked for this meeting to request the terms of our surrender.
All I ask is that your men lay down their arms.
Agreed. Shall we put the conditions on paper?
Allowing my men to keep their horses is very generous. They will need the animals when they return to their farms.

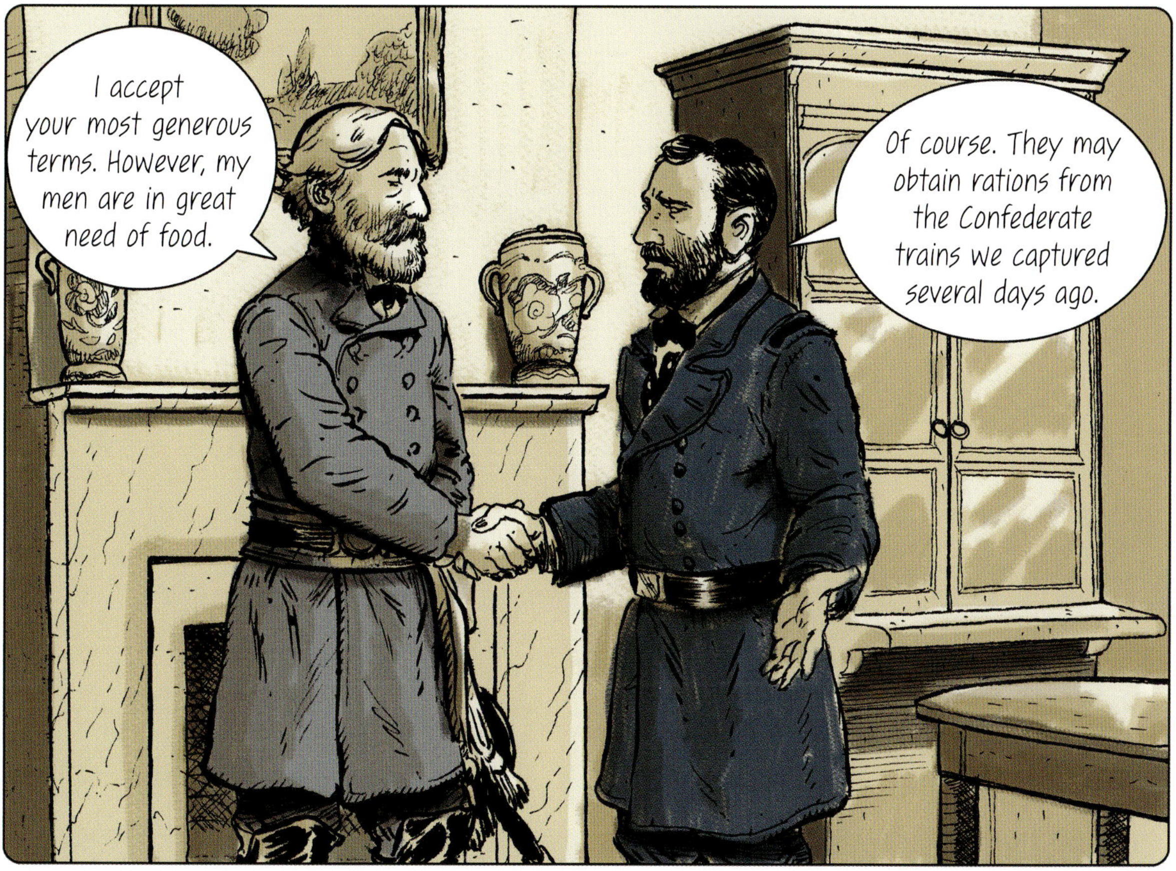
I accept your most generous terms. However, my men are in great need of food.
Of course. They may obtain rations from the Confederate trains we captured several days ago.

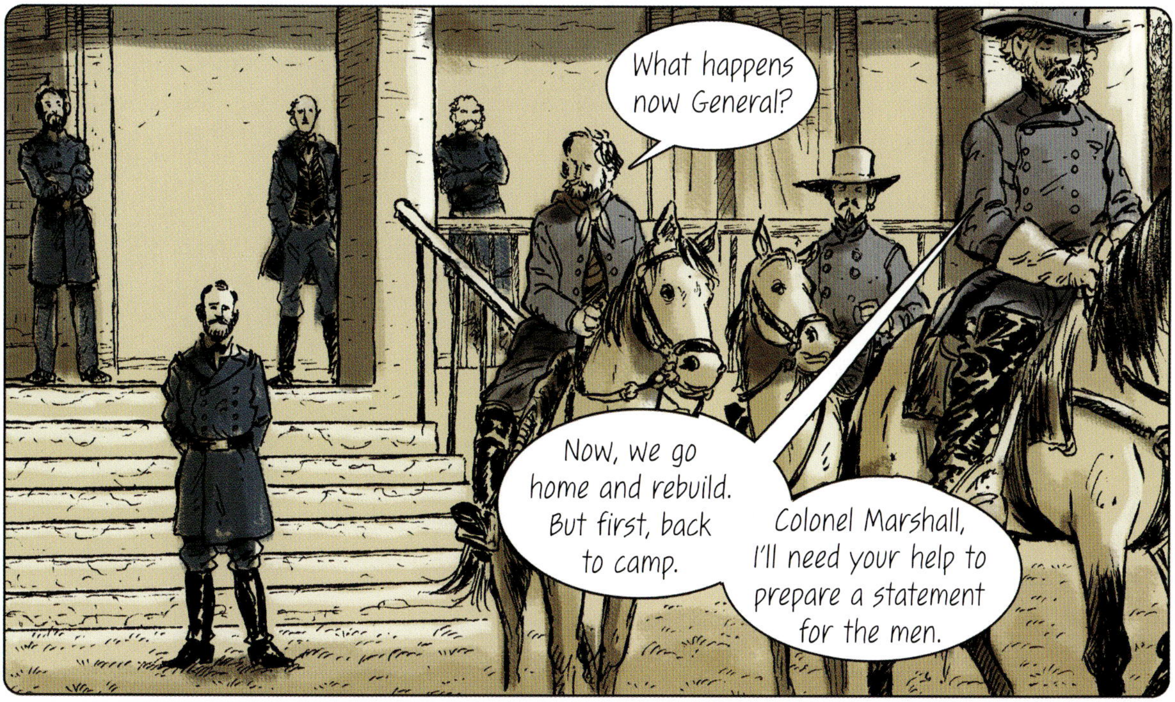
What happens now General?
Now, we go home and rebuild. But first, back to camp.
Colonel Marshall, I'll need your help to prepare a statement for the men.

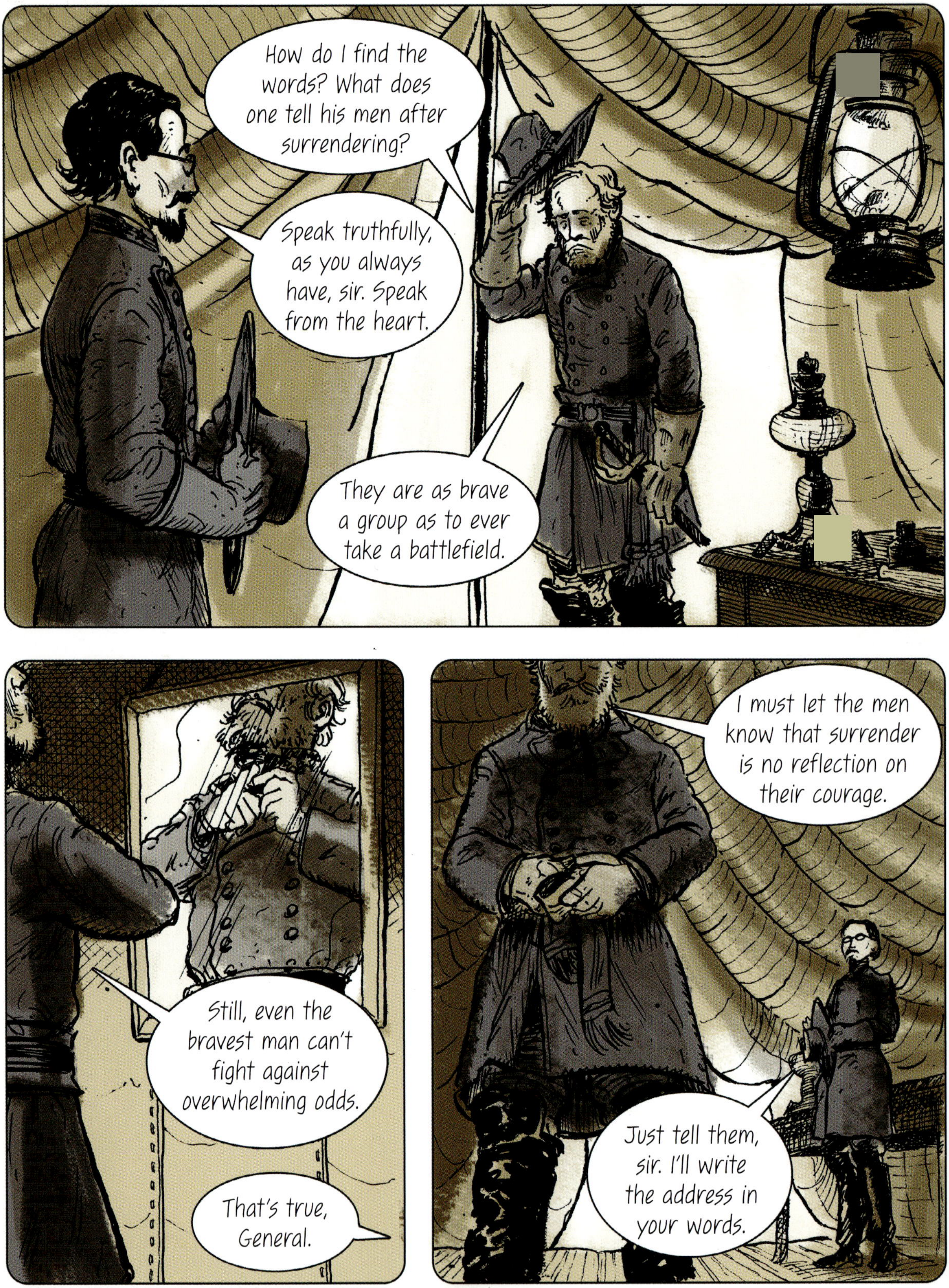
How do I find the words? What does one tell his men after surrendering?
Speak truthfully, as you always have, sir. Speak from the heart.
They are as brave a group as to ever take a battlefield.
Still, even the bravest man can't fight against overwhelming odds.
That's true, General.
I must let the men know that surrender is no reflection on their courage.
Just tell them, sir. I'll write the address in your words.

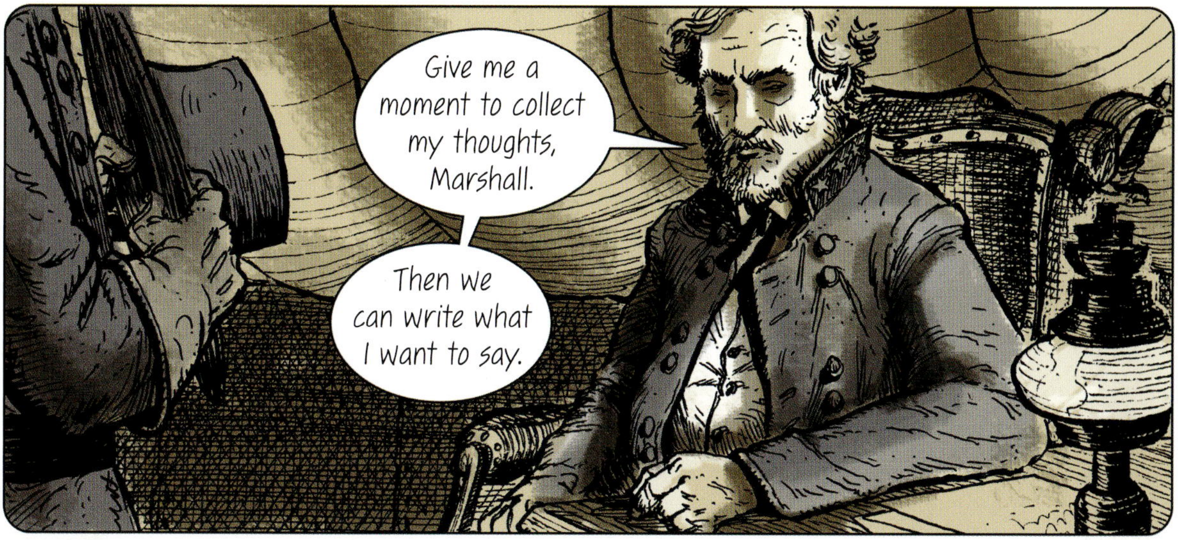
Give me a moment to collect my thoughts, Marshall.
Then we can write what I want to say.

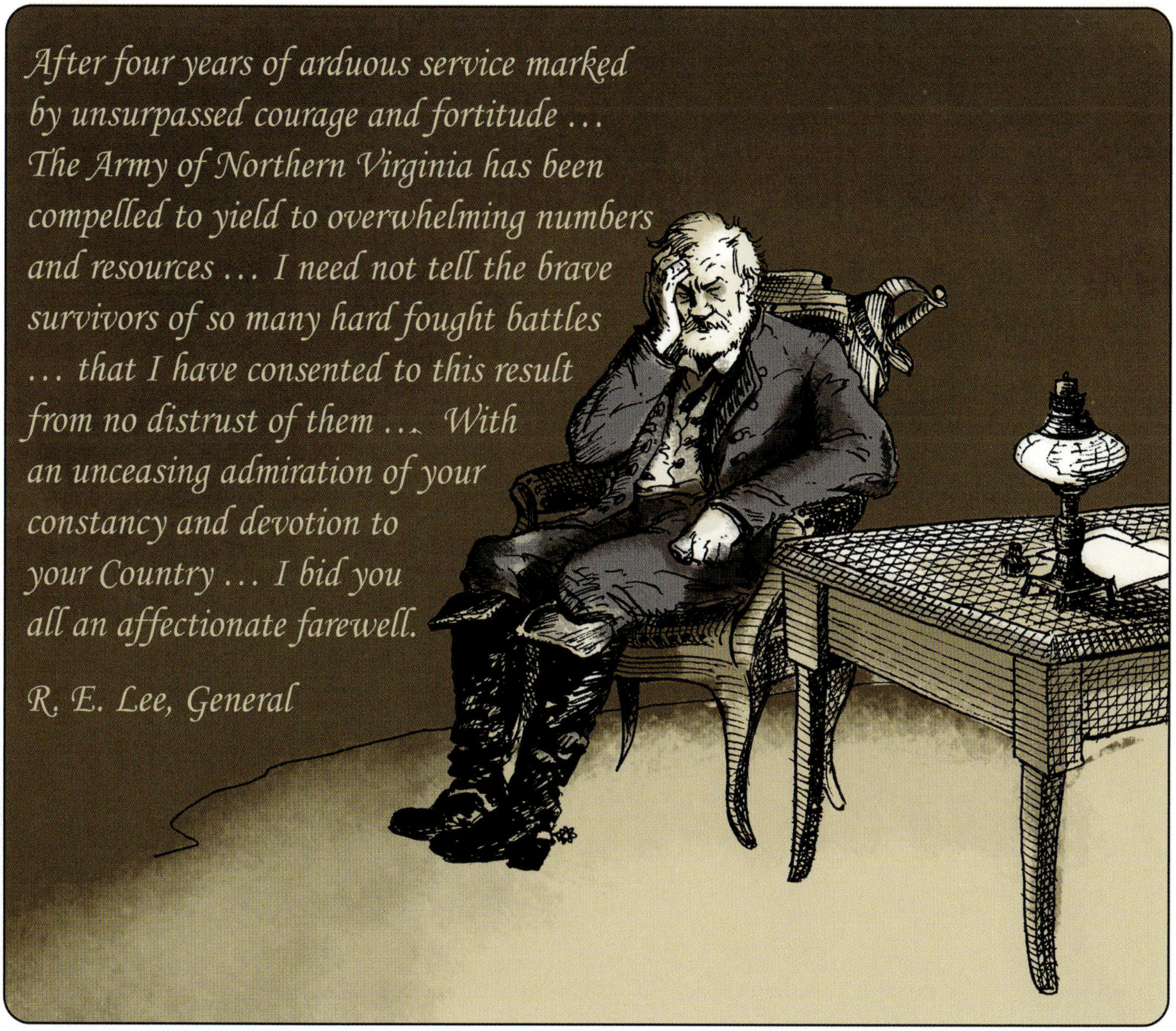
After four years of arduous service marked by unsurpassed courage and fortitude … The Army of Northern Virginia has been compelled to yield to overwhelming numbers and resources … I need not tell the brave survivors of so many hard fought battles … that I have consented to this result from no distrust of them … With an unceasing admiration of your constancy and devotion to your Country … I bid you all an affectionate farewell.
R. E. Lee, General

THE LEGACY OF ROBERT E. LEE

Robert Edward Lee was born in Stratford, Virginia on January 19, 1807. Lee's father Henry was a Revolutionary War cavalry commander and later the governor of Virginia. Lee grew up in a household where serving the public good was a natural calling. He chose to serve the United States by attending the U.S. Military Academy at West Point. He graduated second in class in 1829, and became an engineer in the U.S. Army.

In 1831 he married Mary Custis and later fathered four daughters and three sons. All of his sons later served as officers in the Confederate Army. Lee fought in the Mexican-American War from 1846 to 1848. From September, 1852 to March, 1855, he served as the superintendant at West Point. Later in 1855 he transferred to the calvary to fight Indians in Texas.

At the outbreak of the Civil War, Lee resigned his commission in the U.S. Army. He fully intended to stay out of the conflict. Lee disliked slavery and opposed secession from the Union. He hoped to avoid becoming entangled in the war. However, once his home state of Virginia seceded from the Union, he agreed to join the Confederacy. Ultimately, he became General in Chief of the Confederate Army. Lee also acted as military advisor to Confederate President Jefferson Davis.

After the surrender at Appomattox Court House, Lee went home to live out the rest of his life in peace. He accepted the presidency of Washington College at Lexington, Virginia. He oversaw the rebuilding of the college after the devastation of the war. He was a popular figure on campus, where he lived and served until his death on October 12, 1870.

MILESTONES OF ROBERT E. LEE'S LIFE

1825–1829:
Attended West Point

1846–1848:
Fought in Mexican-American War

1852–1855:
Superintendant at West Point

1862–1864:
Commander, Army of Northern Virginia

1865:
General in Chief of the Confederate Army

1865–1870:
President of Washington College

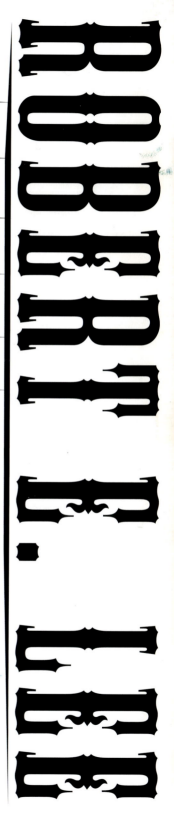

GLOSSARY

ammunition (am-yuh-NI-shuhn)—bullets and other objects that can be fired from weapons

amputate (AM-pyuh-tayt)—to cut off someone's arm, leg, or other body part, usually because the part is damaged beyond repair

brigade (bri-GAYD)—a unit of soldiers that includes two or more regiments

casualty (KAZH-oo-uhl-tee)—someone who is injured, captured, killed, or missing in battle

cavalry (KA-vuhl-ree)—soldiers trained to travel and fight on horseback

Confederacy (kuhn-FE-druh-see)—the 11 southern states that left the United States to form the Confederate States of America

earthwork (URTH-wurk)—a military construction made mainly of dirt for protection against enemy fire

flank (FLANGK)—to move around the right or left side of a military formation

infantry (IN-fuhn-tree)—soldiers trained to travel and fight on foot

pneumonia (noo-MOH-nyuh)—a serious disease that infects the lungs, causing them to fill with thick fluid and make breathing difficult

ration (RASH-uhn)—a soldier's daily share of food

secede (si-SEED)—to formally withdraw from a group or organization; the Confederate states seceded from the United States at the time of the Civil War

strategy (STRAT-uh-jee)—a plan for winning a military battle or achieving a goal

surrender (suh-REN-dur)—to give up or admit defeat

tactic (TAK-tik)—a plan for fighting a battle

Union (YOON-yuhn)—the states that remained loyal to the United States during the Civil War

READ MORE

McLeese, Don. *Robert E. Lee.* Military Leaders of the Civil War. Vero Beach, Fla.: Rourke, 2006.

Ransom, Candice F. *Robert E. Lee.* History Maker Bios. Minneapolis: Lerner Publications Co., 2005.

Vander Hook, Sue. *Confederate Commander: General Robert E. Lee.* We the People. Minneapolis: Compass Point Books, 2009.

INTERNET SITES

FactHound offers a safe, fun way to find Internet sites related to this book. All of the sites on FactHound have been researched by our staff.

Here's all you do: Visit www.facthound.com

Type in this code: 9781429654753

Super-cool stuff!

Check out projects, games and lots more at
www.capstonekids.com

31

INDEX

AMERICAN GRAPHIC

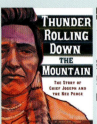